MASON AND DIXON'S
LINE OF FIRE

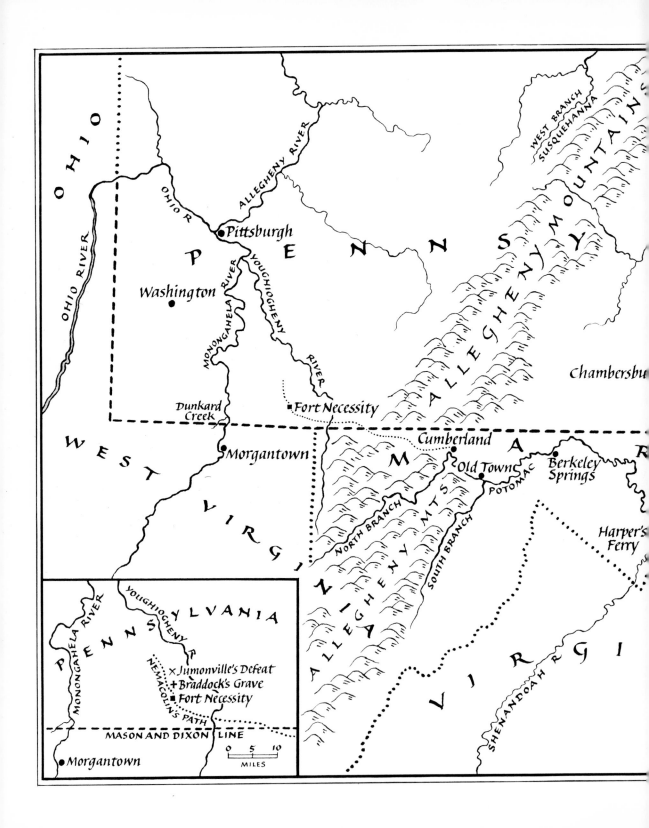

OHIO

OHIO RIVER

ALLEGHENY RIVER

OHIO R.

● Pittsburgh

P E N N S Y L V A N I A

Washington ●

MONONGAHELA RIVER

YOUGHIOGHENY RIVER

WEST BRANCH SUSQUEHANNA

A L L E G H E N Y   M O U N T A I N S

Chambersb...

Dunkard
Creek

■ Fort Necessity

W E S T

● Morgantown

Cumberland ●

Old Town ●

● Berkeley
Springs

POTOMAC

M A

R

V I R G I N I A

NORTH BRANCH

SOUTH BRANCH

A L L E G H E N Y   M T S

Harper's
Ferry

V I R G I

SHENANDOAH R.

P E N N S Y L V A N I A

MONONGAHELA RIVER

YOUGHIOGHENY

NEMACOLIN'S PATH

× Jumonville's Defeat
+ Braddock's Grave
■ Fort Necessity

MASON AND DIXON LINE

● Morgantown

0   5   10
MILES

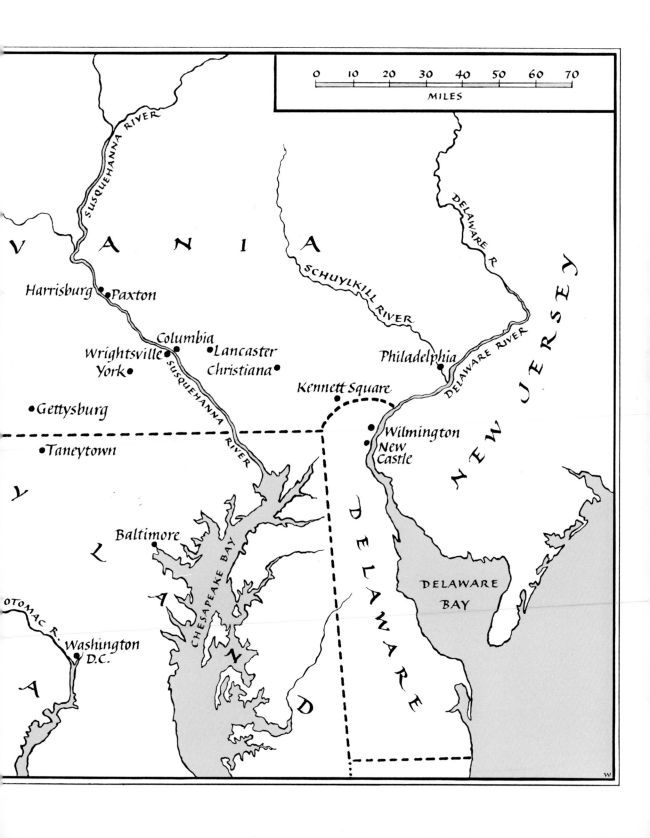

JUDITH ST. GEORGE

MASON AND DIXON'S LINE OF FIRE

illustrated with photographs, prints and maps

G.P. PUTNAM'S SONS   NEW YORK

G. P. Putnam's Sons, a division of The Putnam & Grosset Book Group,
200 Madison Avenue, New York, NY 10016.
Published simultaneously in Canada.
Printed in the United States of America.
Book design by Kathleen Westray

Library of Congress Cataloging-in-Publication Data
St. George, Judith
Mason and Dixon's line of fire / Judith St. George :
illustrated with photographs, prints, and maps. p.   cm.
Includes bibliographical references and index.
Summary: Tells the story of the sometimes violent boundary
disputes between colonial Maryland and Pennsylvania, and how
two surveyors established the line that finally brought peace.
1. Mason-Dixon Line—Juvenile literature.   [1. Mason-Dixon Line.]
I. Title. F157.B7S8 1991 974.8'802—dc20 90-21625 CIP AC
1   3   5   7   9   10   8   6   4   2
ISBN 0-399-22240-5

First Impression

CONTENTS

1763
November
8 15ᵗ # Arived at Philadelphia.

16 Attended a meeting of the Commissioners appointed by the
Proprietors of Pensylvania to settle the boundaries of the Province.

17 Wrote to his Excellency Horatio Sharpe Esqʳ Governour of
Maryland, signifying our arrival at Philadelphia.

22 Landed the Instruments.

25 Set up the Sector } and found they had not receiv'd
28 Set up the Transit } any damage.

30 The Commissioners appointed by Lord Baltimore to settle the
Boundaries of Maryland came to Philadelphia. ——————

Decem 1ˢᵗ Attended a meeting of the Commissioners of both Provinces;
and set up the Compound Instrument of Lord Baltimore's.

2ᵈ Attended a meeting of the Commissioners.

3ᵈ Attended Dᵒ

5ᵗʰ Attended Dᵒ and directed a carpenter to build an Observatory
near the Point settled by the Commissioners to be the South end of the
City of Philadelphia.

6 Set up a Sector brought by the Commissioners from Maryland,
and found the Screws would not touch the middle part of the Arch.
Was sworn before the Commissioners. ——————

7 Attended the Commissioners.

8 Carried some of our Instruments into the Observatory.

9 Attended the Commissioners, and received our Instructions.

10 }
11 } Got the Observatory finish'd and fixd up our Instruments
12 } proper for observing.
13 }

14 Rain & Snow

15 Dᵒ

8.

"ARRIVED AT PHILADELPHIA," Charles Mason wrote in his journal on November 15, 1763, as he and Jeremiah Dixon landed in the largest and wealthiest city in the American colonies. The names Mason and Dixon are known to almost everyone, but who they were, and what they did, isn't so well-known.

Charles Mason and Jeremiah Dixon were two English scientists who were hired in 1763 to survey the boundary line that separated Maryland and Pennsylvania. Little did they guess that in the years to come, their names, and the line that they were to survey, would become legendary. If they had known, perhaps they would have had their portraits painted, but no likeness of either man has ever been found.

Luckily, there is a complete record of Mason and Dixon's five years in America. Charles Mason kept a daily journal beginning with their 1763 arrival and ending with their 1768 return to England. Although the entries are mostly technical, around the edges of the scientific data there are revealing glimpses of Mason and Dixon's remarkable American adventure.

Actually, the story of Mason and Dixon's line began long before the two Englishmen started their survey and lasted long after they had finished. It was as if the line itself sparked flames of violence, as it became a battleground for quarrels, massacres, rebellions, wars, narrow escapes and natural disasters. For more than two hundred years, Mason and Dixon's line has stood as a metaphor for how our country and its people have faced adversity and hardship with courage and determination . . . and endured.

Charles Mason begins his journal as soon as he arrives in Philadelphia on November 15, 1763.

CHAPTER 1

THE MARYLAND
MONSTER

A strange little war broke out in the American colonies in the 1730s. The strange little war even had a name, the Conojacular War. And right in the middle of that war was Thomas Cresap.

If the expression "rugged frontiersman" could be used to describe anyone, it could be used to describe Thomas Cresap. A hot-tempered Englishman, Cresap was one of thousands of hardy immigrants who sailed to America determined to make their mark in the new world. As a young man, Cresap settled in the Conojohary Valley at Wright's Ferry (now Wrightsville, Pennsylvania) on land that was granted to him in 1730 by the government of Maryland. There, on the west bank of the Susquehanna River, he began a ferry service transporting people, livestock and cargo across the river to the village of Columbia. And it was there that Thomas Cresap began the Conojacular War.

In the days when England ruled the American colonies, each

A horse and carriage are ferried across the Susquehanna River.

colony or province was like a separate nation. Like neighboring nations, neighboring provinces quarreled about almost everything, especially about where their boundary lines ran. In the Conojohary Valley, settlers like Thomas Cresap, who had been granted land by the government of Maryland, insisted that they lived in Maryland. On the other hand, those settlers in the Conojohary Valley who had been granted land by Pennsylvania argued that they lived in Pennsylvania. (The arguing didn't end until Mason and Dixon surveyed and established the exact boundary line in the 1760s.)

To be fair, the settlers weren't entirely to blame. In 1632, the province of Maryland had been granted to Lord Baltimore by the King of England (King Charles I). Some fifty years later, in 1681, the province of Pennsylvania was granted to William Penn by King Charles II. Because royalty tended to be careless and maps in the 17th century weren't very accurate, the Baltimores and the Penns both claimed the same strip of land on the Maryland-Pennsylvania border, as well as the same section of Philadelphia. Furthermore, the Baltimores and the Penns both claimed the right to collect rent and tax money from the settlers who lived along that border.

Years of arguing between the Baltimores and the Penns followed. At least the Baltimores and the Penns argued with words. The settlers argued, too, only they argued with guns . . . especially that rugged frontiersman, Thomas Cresap.

Much to the annoyance of his Pennsylvania neighbors, right from the beginning, Thomas Cresap declared that he lived in Maryland. By October of 1730, Cresap had provoked his neighbors to the point that two Pennsylvanians whom he was ferrying across the river suddenly pulled out their guns. "Damn you Cresap turn to shore or you are a dead man," one of them ordered. The two Pennsylvanians couldn't have known Cresap very well. Although they stunned him with a blow from a gun butt, Cresap wasn't down for long. Swinging at one of the gunmen with an oar, Cresap wrestled him to the bottom of the boat.

Lord Baltimore and his
grandson holding a map
of Maryland.

It was only after a furious struggle that the two Pennsylvanians were able to throw Cresap into the water. Holding on to the boat, Cresap kept the men arguing until he could feel the river bottom under his feet, whereupon he gave the boat a mighty shove. As the boat drifted downstream, Cresap half-walked, half-swam to a small island in the middle of the mile-wide river, where he waited to be rescued. And with that incident, the Conojacular War of the 1730s began.

Before long there was so much trouble between Cresap and his Pennsylvania neighbors that the governors of both provinces jumped into the controversy. A provincial governor was the agent of the English crown who represented the king and commanded the province's militia. The governor of Maryland, Samuel Ogle, complained to Pennsylvania's Governor Patrick Gordon that Cresap had been badly mistreated by his neighbors. Governor Gordon, in turn, replied that the affair was nothing but a quarrel between a few Pennsylvanians, with Cresap foolishly calling himself a Marylander.

In 1732, Cresap, who was hardly an innocent party to the trouble, shot and killed a number of his neighbors' cattle and horses on the grounds that they had been allowed to run loose in his cornfield and destroy his crops. The following year, twenty Pennsylvanians surrounded Cresap's cabin and threatened to hang him, as well as anyone else who took over land in Pennsylvania under grants from Maryland. When the mob broke down the door, Cresap and several Marylanders who were hiding in the house opened fire. Although they wounded one of the attackers, before the fighting was over, the Pennsylvania mob beat up Cresap and his companions.

In January of 1734, Thomas Cresap, who by now was known throughout Pennsylvania as the Maryland Monster, tried to parcel off land to Maryland settlers that already belonged to Pennsylvanians. This was too much for the Lancaster County sheriff, who organized a posse and set out to arrest Cresap. Having been warned of the posse's approach, Cresap and his Maryland friends again armed themselves and assembled in the Cresaps' fortified log cabin.

As soon as the sheriff and his men arrived, Cresap shouted through the door that they should "Look between the Logs and they might Se [See] Eleven Guns more, which they shoud have the Guts of it if they stayed there." Although two of the posse were able to force their way into the house, they "soon returned bruised and Bloody." In the gunfire that followed, one of the sheriff's posse, Knowles Daunt, was wounded. When Mrs. Cresap, who was as hotheaded as her husband, was asked to help the wounded Daunt, she not only refused but also called out that she was sorry that he had only a leg wound. She "had rather itt had been his heart." (Daunt died of his wounds soon afterwards.)

By now the tone of the letters between the two governors was growing sharper. Pennsylvania's Governor Gordon described Cre-

Even a well-fortified log cabin isn't much more than a one-room, one-window shack.

sap as a "publick Disturber of the Peace of both Governments," while Maryland's Governor Ogle retorted (rather questionably) that Cresap "is a very sober and modest Person, and has been particularly careful . . . to give no Offence to any Person under your Government." It didn't help when Governor Ogle added that he also counted on Cresap to "defend himself in Case any unjust attack should be made upon him."

Cresap didn't wait long to take Governor Ogle at his word. In May of 1736, Cresap's Pennsylvania neighbors were astounded to see a surveyor, accompanied by Cresap and twenty armed men, surveying land along the Susquehanna River that already belonged to Pennsylvania Dutch farmers. Cresap, who had just been made a captain in the Maryland militia, warned the Pennsylvanians that he would "shoot the first man that should molest the Surveyor."

At Cresap's latest outrage, the furious Pennsylvania authorities ordered Cresap's arrest for the murder of Knowles Daunt. Samuel Smith, the new sheriff of Lancaster County, surrounded Cresap's house at daybreak on November 24, 1736, with a twenty-four-man posse and an arrest warrant. Sheriff Smith later reported that Cresap responded to the warrant "with several horrid Oaths and the most abusive Language . . . that they should never have him till he was a Corpse, and filling a glass of Rum he drank Damnation to himself and all that were with him if ever he or they surrendered."

Cresap's version of the incident was somewhat different. "My answer was that as I was in my Own House which I Thought my Castle, Neither the Laws of God or Man would Compell me to Surrender." Whichever account was accurate, both versions made clear that Cresap had no intention of giving himself up.

Realizing that Cresap would never surrender, the posse set fire to a shed next to Cresap's log cabin. The flames quickly spread, forcing Cresap, and everyone inside, to flee the burning building. As shots rang out, Cresap and two of the posse were wounded, with the sheriff's men fatally wounding Cresap's loyal servant, who had earlier sworn that he would "rather lose his Life than to be False to his [Cresap's] trust." Cresap later testified: "Several Guns were fired Several of which shots hit me perticularly one in my shoulder, three small shott on my middle finger, and one on my right Eye brow."

Wounded or not, Cresap ran out the back door and down to the dock to escape across the Susquehanna River. But as he fumbled with his boatline, the sheriff's men overtook and captured him. Even under arrest, and with his hands tied, the wounded Cresap managed to elbow one of his captors overboard on the ride across the river. As soon as they landed on the opposite shore, Sheriff Smith had a blacksmith fit Cresap's wrists with irons. But no irons could hold the Maryland Monster, who raised his shackled hands above his head and with one blow knocked the startled blacksmith to the ground.

As Cresap was marched "in Irons" through Philadelphia on his way to jail, crowds gathered in the streets, doorways and windows to get a glimpse of the notorious Maryland Monster. Taking advantage of all the attention, Cresap turned to his guard and announced loudly: "Damn it, Ashton, this is one of the Prettyest towns in Maryland."

Even in prison, Cresap stayed true to form, making so much trouble that his exasperated jailers finally told him that he was free to go. But Cresap refused the offer on the grounds that his king hadn't ordered it. At last, on August 18, 1737, King George II commanded that no more grants of land be made by either province along the Maryland-Pennsylvania boundary line, nor were "any Tumults, Riots, or other Outrageous Disorders to be Committed on the Borders." With that proclamation, the Conojacular War was over and the Maryland Monster, after serving eight months in prison, was released, no doubt to the great relief of his jailers.

With his house burned to the ground and with further fighting forbidden by the king, Thomas Cresap moved west. He, his wife and five children first settled on an Indian warpath just south of the Maryland-Pennsylvania border. But apparently even an Indian warpath wasn't challenge enough for Cresap. Three years later, in

1740, he moved his family to an abandoned Indian village called Shawnee Old Town (now Oldtown, Maryland), farther west than any other white settlement. (The Allegheny Mountains served as the country's westernmost frontier until after the American Revolution.) It was there, on the crossroads of an Indian travel route, that Thomas Cresap lived for more than fifty years, acquiring the kind of independence and prosperity that he had come to America to find.

Rogue that he was, larger-than-life Thomas Cresap expressed the kind of spirit and will that opened up the American frontier. Boundaries couldn't hold back these headstrong new Americans. They would live where they pleased, as they pleased. The half-serious, half-comic Conojacular War that pitted neighbor against neighbor expressed the new America, too. With boundary lines inaccurate and poorly drawn, settlers everywhere were quick to take up arms to defend their homes and property. Unfortunately, the end of the Conojacular War didn't mark the end of violence along the Maryland-Pennsylvania border. It was only the first of many fires that would ignite, flare up, burn and die down, only to burst into flames somewhere else.

Thomas Cresap's fortified cabin is built on a bluff.

DEFEAT IN THE WILDERNESS

Much of George Washington's youth was spent along the western Maryland-Pennsylvania border country at a time when Great Britain still ruled the American colonies. During those early years, George Washington not only learned how to survive in the wilderness, but he also observed how the woodland Indians lived . . . and fought. It was knowledge that he would draw on in the years to come. Although he would meet with two devastating defeats on that Maryland-Pennsylvania frontier, those defeats would season and shape the young Washington into the leader that he would one day become.

Because Washington had always been good at math and geography, working as a surveyor appealed to him. (Surveyors determine the shape and area of any part of the earth's surface so that maps can be drawn or boundaries established.) It was as a sixteen-year-old surveyor's assistant that Washington first met Thomas Cresap. Traveling to Old Town, Maryland, in 1748, Washington spent

four nights with Cresap, who had recently been promoted to colonel in the Maryland militia. "We went over in a Canoe and travell'd up Maryland side all the Day in a Continued Rain to Collo Cresaps," Washington complained in his journal. "I believe the worst Road that ever was trod by Man or Beast."

Six years later, in 1754, Washington returned to the Maryland-Pennsylvania border country, this time on a military assignment. A great admirer of his half-brother, Lawrence, who had served in the military, Washington had joined the colonial Virginia militia when he was twenty. (The militia was made up of part-time colonial soldiers in contrast to the full-time professional British soldiers who served in the British army.) In April of 1754, twenty-two-year-old Lieutenant Colonel Washington arrived at Wills Creek, Maryland, at the head of 150 Virginia militiamen. The small force was on its way to defend a fort being built by the British at the Forks of the Ohio, where the Allegheny River joins the Monongahela River to form the Ohio River (the site of present-day Pittsburgh).

At Wills Creek, which was only a few miles south of the Maryland-Pennsylvania border, Washington picked up supplies at the Ohio Company's New Storehouse which was being managed by Thomas Cresap. While there, Washington was alarmed to learn that French soldiers and their Indian allies had already captured the half-finished British fort at the Forks of the Ohio. "Came down to Colonel Cresap's," Washington wrote in his journal, "and on my route, had noticed that the fort was taken by the French." In its place, the French were building a much larger fort, which they were calling Fort Duquesne.

Although England and France had been at war in North America on and off for 65 years, in the Spring of 1754, no official state of war existed between them. Nevertheless, tensions ran high, with both England and France claiming the rich Ohio Valley, the present states of Ohio, Indiana, Illinois, Kentucky and Tennessee.

Determined to continue on to the Forks of the Ohio, Washington sent back to Virginia for reinforcements before leading his

As a surveyor's assistant, the young George Washington holds a scope and a measuring chain.

men out of Wills Creek on April 29, 1754. Following Nemacolin's Path, a twelve-foot-wide trail that Thomas Cresap and the Indian Nemacolin had blazed three years before, Washington marched his troops north across the Maryland-Pennsylvania border.

On May 23, Washington halted his men just over the border in a large clearing called Great Meadows where they set up camp. Bad news reached Washington several days later when his Indian scout, the Half-King, reported that thirty-three French soldiers had been camped in hiding for two days on Laurel Hill only a few miles from Great Meadows.

If the French soldiers were on a friendly mission, Washington reasoned, they would have made their presence known immediately instead of remaining undercover. No, the French must be spying on him and his men! Then and there, Washington made up his mind to storm the French encampment. Traveling to the Half-King's camp, Washington later noted: ". . . after holding a council with the *Half-King,* we concluded to attack them [the French] together."

At dawn on May 28, 1754, Washington, his men, the Half-King and a party of braves silently surrounded the rocky glen on Laurel Hill where the sleeping French soldiers were camped. In a swift victory, Washington and his forces killed ten Frenchmen, including their commanding officer, the Sieur de Jumonville, wounded one soldier and took the other twenty-one soldiers prisoner. "I can with much truth assure you, I heard Bulletts whistle and believe me there was something charming in the sound," Washington confessed in a letter to his brother after this, his first battle.

But instead of meekly surrendering, Washington's captives were openly defiant. Through an interpreter, the French soldiers argued that they had been on a peaceful diplomatic mission to deliver a letter to the British. With the death of their commanding officer, Jumonville, they charged Washington with the murder of an innocent ambassador.

Washington, who didn't believe their story for a minute, brushed aside their angry protests. Certain that French troops

George Washington is a colonel in the Virginia militia when his first portrait is painted.

Lieutenant Colonel George Washington confers with the Half-King before attacking the French.

from Fort Duquesne would come after him as soon as they heard of his surprise attack, Washington ordered his men, plus the two hundred reinforcements who had just arrived, to build a fort in the middle of Great Meadows, which he called Fort Necessity.

Because Indian tribes were small and every warrior was needed to provide both food and protection, Indians simply deserted when they were outnumbered or when a battle appeared hopeless. Foreseeing disaster at the hands of the French, the Half-King and his followers packed up their camp and silently disappeared. Pennsylvania's Indian agent later reported that "the Half-King complained . . . that Colonel Washington had made no fortifications at all, but that little thing upon the meadow."

The Half-King was right. Fort Necessity, "that little thing upon the meadow," was not only too small to shelter all of Washington's forces, but it was also located in a marshy valley surrounded by wooded hills that would provide perfect cover for attacking troops. Furthermore, food and ammunition were running low and one fourth of Washington's men were sick.

The French troops, who marched down from Fort Duquesne to avenge the British attack just as Washington had predicted, quickly surrounded Fort Necessity. In an eight-hour battle that was fought in the pouring rain, the French overpowered the fort and captured its defenders. But rather than taking Washington and his men prisoner, the French announced that if Washington signed a document (written in French), he would be allowed to march his troops away with full honors of war.

Fort Necessity is situated in a low valley surrounded by wooded hills.

With thirty of his men dead and seventy wounded, Washington knew that he had little choice. After signing the document, a humiliated Washington led his forces out of the mud and muck of Great Meadows to the beat of drums and the flutter of waving flags back across the Maryland-Pennsylvania border to Wills Creek. He would never forget the date, the fourth of July, 1754.

In Europe, neither the British nor the French found the whistle of Washington's bullets charming. Possibly Washington's interpreter hadn't translated the French document accurately, but the surrender that Washington had signed stated that the French had never intended "to trouble the Peace and good Harmony" between England and France. They had attacked Fort Necessity, not as a military action, but to "revenge the Assassination" of their ambassador, Jumonville.

Even though Washington was an officer in the Virginia militia, he was, nevertheless, a British subject serving under the British military. By signing the French papers, he had, at one stroke, branded the British Crown as being the aggressor, as well as being responsible for the murder of an ambassador on a peaceful mission. A furious English statesman wrote that the document was "the most infamous a British subject ever put his hand to." The commander of the victorious French force, who was the half-brother of "Ambassador" Jumonville, boasted, "We made the *English* consent to sign, that they had assassinated my Brother in his own Camp."

Although England and France didn't formally declare war in Europe until May 1756, it was there, in the wilderness along the Maryland-Pennsylvania border, that George Washington fired the opening shot of the French and Indian War. For the next nine years, England and France would battle for control of North America.

It was during the first year of that war, in June of 1755, that Washington once again found himself in the western border country of Maryland and Pennsylvania. This time he was accompanying 1,000 British regulars and 1,500 colonial militiamen under the command of British General Edward Braddock. Having received good reports about the young colonial officer, Braddock had invited Washington to become a member of his staff. Although Washington had resigned from the Virginia militia after his defeat at Fort Necessity, he had accepted the offer to serve as Braddock's unpaid and unofficial aide-de-camp.

Braddock, whose mission was to capture Fort Duquesne from the French, planned a brief stopover to pick up supplies at Thomas Cresap's New Storehouse. Arriving in a splendid coach at Fort Cumberland, Maryland, which had been built by the British at Wills Creek after the fall of Fort Necessity, the arrogant Braddock made clear that he had little use for the colonial militia and even less use for Thomas Cresap. In his dealings with Cresap, Braddock complained that he had been "deceived and met with nothing but Lies and Villiany." Apparently his fellow British officers felt the same way, referring to Cresap as "that Rattle Snake Colonel" and "a vile Rascal."

Fort Cumberland is built to serve as a defense on the western frontier.

After impatiently waiting a month for the supplies that had been ordered, Braddock, Washington and the troops finally started out from Fort Cumberland on June 10, 1755. Three hundred axmen led the way north on Nemacolin's Path, cutting down trees to widen the trail for the passage of cannons and wagons. During the second week of difficult travel over the Allegheny Mountains, Washington fell seriously ill and had to drop behind.

Still feeling "very low and weak," Washington didn't overtake the army until July 7th. Only two days later, he was riding with Braddock and an advance guard of 1,200 handpicked men through a heavily wooded area on a narrow trail, when there sounded the bloodcurdling shriek of Indian war whoops and the volley of gunfire. The French and their Indian allies had surrounded the British in an ambush!

Hiding behind trees and fallen logs, the French and Indians fired into the packed masses of British soldiers and militiamen. What had been a disciplined army quickly became a panicked mob. The advance guard, shooting wildly, stampeded to the rear at the same time that the main body of the army pressed forward.

As Braddock's aide, Washington begged the British general to allow his men to scatter and fight Indian-style from behind cover. But Braddock refused, commanding his troops to maintain their traditional rigid formation. "Stand and fight!" he bellowed. The result was a slaughter. Two-thirds of Braddock's forces were killed, wounded or taken prisoner in the worst defeat that the British suffered in all their years of North American rule.

Only Washington and his colonial militiamen emerged from the disaster with honor. Washington, who "had four bullets pass through my coat, and two horses shot out from under me," declared that the militia "behaved like men and died like soldiers." On the other hand, he had nothing but contempt for the British regulars, who "broke and ran as sheep before hounds."

With a bullet lodged in his lungs, General Braddock was carried from the field and transported back along Nemacolin's Path in a cart. "Who would have thought it?" he moaned. Washington had

been right, he admitted. "We shall better know how to deal with them next time."

But there would be no next time for Braddock. He died four days after the battle. Familiar with Indian practices, Washington had Braddock buried on the trail and then ordered troops and horse-drawn wagons to pass over the grave so that the Indians couldn't find the body and mutilate it. And where was that grave? It was only a few miles north of the Maryland-Pennsylvania border on Nemacolin's Path, close by the ruins of Fort Necessity.

The dying British General Braddock is carried in a cart back along Nemacolin's Path after the French and Indians defeat his army in an ambush.

Just as England and France focused on America's western frontier during the 1750s, so too did the American colonies focus on the tall, lanky colonial colonel from Virginia. The young George Washington, whose military career would span more than forty years, was tempered and hardened by his failures in the mountains along the Maryland-Pennsylvania border. The colonies were tempered and hardened by those events, too. The famed British regulars had been slashed to ribbons in a wilderness battle for which they had been unsuited and unprepared. It was a lesson that George Washington, and the thirteen colonies, would well remember in the years ahead.

George Washington reads the burial service before General Braddock is buried on Nemacolin's Path.

CHAPTER 3

BLOOD ON
THE MOON

F ollowing General Braddock's defeat and death at the hands of
the French and Indians in July of 1755, what was left of the
British Army retreated in total confusion across the border from
Pennsylvania to Fort Cumberland, Maryland. From there, George
Washington returned to Virginia, while the shattered British
Army fled to Philadelphia and their winter quarters . . . on August
second! Quick to take advantage of the British retreat that left the
frontier settlements unprotected, the French ordered their Indian
allies to stop at nothing to drive out the English.

The western wilderness, homeland to many tribes, had been
prime Indian hunting grounds until the English began cutting
down the trees, fencing in the land and killing or driving away
the game. Now the Indians seized the opportunity to regain what
they considered to be rightfully theirs. In the late summer and fall
of 1755, Indian war parties raided the western border country of
Maryland, Pennsylvania and Virginia, killing and scalping men,

women and children, carrying off captives, butchering livestock and burning houses and barns. Hardly a night passed when there wasn't "blood on the moon."

The settlers, who had existed side by side with the Indians for years, were unprepared for the violence. When the Quaker William Penn had arrived in Philadelphia in 1682, he had drawn up a friendship treaty with the Indians that had resulted in more than seventy years of peace. But during those same seventy years, ever-growing numbers of settlers had taken over more and more Indian territory. With the outbreak of the French and Indian War, even the once-friendly Delawares and Shawnees devastated white settlements.

In October of 1755, Fort Cumberland's commander reported: "Nothing is to be seen or heard but Desolation and Murder. . . . The Smoke of Burning plantations darken the day and hide the neighboring mountains from our sight." A Fort Cumberland sentry described an attacking war party: "The men were tall, greasy, and naked except for breach clouts and deerskin moccasins, their inflexible faces daubed with red, yellow, and black paint. The outer rims of their ears were slit and their tufts of hair stuck with feathers."

Their war cries were equally terrifying. "When we came to the west side of Laurel-Hill," a captive later wrote, "they gave the scalp halloo, as usual, which is a long yell or halloo, for every scalp or prisoner they have in possession; the last of these scalp halloos were followed with quick and sudden shrill shouts of joy and triumph."

By late 1755, Indian scalping parties had struck as far inland as the Susquehanna River, the site of Thomas Cresap's earlier Conojacular War. Although the Indians never reached Philadelphia, its citizens glimpsed first-hand what their fellow Pennsylvanians were suffering on the frontier. Enraged that so little was being done to help them, settlers drove the mutilated bodies of a murdered family through Philadelphia's streets in an open wagon and then left their grisly cargo on the steps of the State House.

George Washington, who was commander in chief of the Virginia militia, as well as commander of Fort Cumberland from 1756 to 1758, described his sense of helplessness: "The supplicating tears of the women, and moving petitions of the men, melt me into such deadly sorrow, that I solemnly declare, if I know my own mind, I could offer myself a willing sacrifice to the butchering enemy, provided that would contribute to the people's case."

On the other hand, the French were delighted. "I have suceeded in ruining the three adjacent provinces, Pennsylvania, Maryland, and Virginia, driving off the inhabitants, and totally destroying the settlements," wrote the French commander of Fort Duquesne. "The Indian villages are full of prisoners of every age and sex. The enemy has lost far more since the battle than on the day of his [Braddock's] defeat."

Upon his arrival in America, William Penn signs a friendship treaty with the Indians of Pennsylvania.

But in the spring of 1756, those settlers who hadn't fled began to rally. They fortified their isolated log cabins, posted sentries while they worked in the fields and set up warning systems in case of attack. They also formed bands of ranging companies that ruthlessly murdered. Armed with tomahawks and scalping knives, and dressed in buckskin and moccasins, the rangers stalked, killed and scalped Indian men, women and children without mercy.

After declaring war on the Delaware Indians in April 1756, Pennsylvania authorities began to build "Indian forts" in seventeen strategic locations. They also offered rewards for the capture or outright murder of any Indian, beginning with a top price of 150 Spanish dollars for a captive Indian male down to 50 Spanish dollars for the scalp of an Indian woman.

Not surprisingly, Thomas Cresap was in the thick of the action. Cresap and his three adult sons were known for their daring, and the Cresaps' well-fortified Old Town house became a refuge for Maryland settlers. But when the number of attacks increased alarmingly, Cresap was forced to move his family some forty miles east to his son Michael's house, which soon became a jumping-off place for raids against the Indians.

In April 1756, Daniel Cresap, Thomas Cresap, Jr., and sixty rangers "dressed and painted like Indians" started on a blood-thirsty expedition "to kill the women and children in the Indian towns, and scalp them, while the warriors are committing the like destruction on our frontiers." Warned of the raid, the Indians escaped, but not before killing Thomas Cresap, Jr., close by where General Braddock had been buried on Nemacolin's Path.

The year 1757 finally brought relief. Soldiers from nearby forts were assigned guard duty to protect the settlers, while the rangers stepped up their attacks, tracking down their prey with packs of dogs. In the end, however, it was the election of William Pitt in 1757 as Great Britain's prime minister that turned the tide.

Prime Minister Pitt ordered thousands of troops, as well as arms and supplies, to be shipped to the American colonies. With the

An Iroquois warrior, wearing snowshoes, carries a deadly club in one hand and wampum in the other, while a fresh scalp dries at the end of his musket.

fall of Fort Duquesne in 1758 and the capture of French-held Montreal in 1760, the French and Indian War in North America was to all intents and purposes over, although France didn't officially surrender to Great Britain until 1763.

However, instead of bringing peace to the Maryland-Pennsylvania-Virginia frontier, the year 1763 ushered in an explosion of violence that matched, or even surpassed, the massacres of the 1750s. By terms of the 1763 Treaty of Paris, France had to turn over all her possessions east of the Mississippi River, except New Orleans, to the English. And the Indians knew only too well what English rule would mean.

The French, who had always treated the Indians as equals, had been interested solely in the fur trade and cared nothing for taking over Indian lands. On the other hand, the English, who despised the Indians as "vermin," destroyed the forests, built permanent homes and cheated the Indians with shoddy goods. The end of the French and Indian War brought about exactly the kind of havoc that the Indians had feared. The English began dividing up the Indian hunting grounds west of the Appalachian Mountains, leaving the Indians "penned up like Hoggs," as one chieftain expressed it. (The Appalachian Mountain Range, which included the Allegheny Mountains, ran the full length of the thirteen colonies.)

In April of 1763, Pontiac, the supreme war chief of the Ottawas, called a meeting of warriors and chieftains from all over the Ohio Valley. A brilliant speaker, Pontiac inflamed the gathering by declaring that it was time to return to the old ways, live as their ancestors had lived and unite against the English, "these dogs dressed in red." As the assembled tribes listened eagerly, a white trader recorded Chief Pontiac's fiery words: "We must exterminate from our land this nation [England] whose only object is our death. We must destroy them without delay. . . . The time has arrived. . . . Let us strike. Strike!"

Strike they did, in a war that became known as Pontiac's Rebellion. Within a month, combined Indian forces attacked and captured all the British forts between the Appalachian Mountains and

BLOOD ON THE MOON   [39]

the Mississippi River, except for Fort Detroit, which they held under siege. Meanwhile, the Delawares and Shawnees seized and burned all the "Indian forts" along Pennsylvania's western frontier, torturing and killing their defenders. Only two forts held out, Fort Pitt, which the British had built on the site of Fort Duquesne, and Fort Niagara in New York. Once again, war parties burned their way across Maryland and Pennsylvania. Once again, wagonloads of bodies rumbled through Philadelphia's cobblestone streets and once again Thomas Cresap became a lightning rod for the violence.

Cresap, whom the Indians called Big Spoon because of the large kettle he kept in his yard for their cooking use, was no longer their friend. This was all-out war and no white man was a friend, certainly not Cresap, who had bought up thousands of acres of Indian land over the years. As he had done in the 1750s, Cresap once again opened his well-stocked log cabin to panicked set-

An old woodcut shows Indians scalping, burning and taking prisoners during a surprise raid.

tlers. But in May of 1763, the Indians put his house under siege. Food and supplies grew scarce. Even the sixth Lord Baltimore in London heard about Cresap's plight. "col: Thomas Cresap with his Family and Neighbors are cut off by the Indians," he wrote to Maryland's governor. "This is Dire!" Finally, in September of 1763, a small force of Maryland militiamen was sent to Old Town to lift the siege on Cresap's house.

Enraged by Indian victories throughout the colonies, the commander of the British forces, General Jeffrey Amherst, sent out orders to treat the Indians "as the vilest race of beings that ever infested the earth." Amherst directed that blankets and clothing from smallpox victims be given to the Indians in hopes of infecting and killing them. All captives were "immediately to be put to death."

Settlers along the Maryland-Pennsylvania border didn't need orders to kill Indians. In December of 1763, a mob of roughnecks from Paxton, Pennsylvania, attacked a band of Conestoga Indians who had lived peacefully for generations in the Susquehanna River area. The Paxton Boys, as they were called, murdered six innocent Conestogas, torched their cabins and paraded their scalps on long sticks. Samuel Smith, the same sheriff who had arrested Thomas Cresap almost thirty years before, locked up the surviving Conestogas in the Lancaster jail for their own protection. Encountering no opposition from the townspeople, the Paxton Boys broke into the jail, killed and scalped fourteen more of the tribe and then rode off in pursuit of the remaining Conestogas, who had fled in terror to Philadelphia. Although the Paxton Boys were prevented from committing any more murders, none of them was ever arrested.

After the death of some 2,000 settlers in only six months, Pontiac's Rebellion began to collapse in the fall of 1763. With Fort Detroit continuing to hold out, and a British victory at Fort Pitt, Pontiac's braves, sensing defeat everywhere, began to return to their homes. Although Pontiac didn't give himself up until 1766, the fighting was essentially over by October of 1763. Pontiac and

his rebellion had held white soldiers at bay longer than any Indian uprising in North American history.

The Maryland-Pennsylvania border country had been a major battleground on which two empires had fought for, and lost control of, a continent. One empire had been the French. The other empire was made up of native Americans who were willing to die for the wilderness where they had lived for thousands of years. Those native Americans not only waged a desperate war on the Maryland-Pennsylvania frontier, but they also waged a desperate war from New England to Georgia, and from the Appalachian Mountains to the Mississippi River. Although they would continue to fight for the next one hundred years to hold on to their lands, in the end their struggle would be futile. The scattered bands of native Americans would prove to be no match for a government, and a people, who believed that it was their "manifest destiny" to occupy the country from coast to coast.

In 1763, the Paxton Boys murder innocent Conestoga Indians . . . and go unpunished.

CHAPTER 4

MILESTONES

After the French and Indian War, the population of the colonies soared as thousands of immigrants from England and Europe sailed to America to find new opportunity. Although land was still plentiful, with the arrival of so many people, the time had come to mark property lines and settle boundary disputes once and for all. Finally, in 1760, after eighty years of arguing, the sixth Lord Baltimore and Thomas and Richard Penn, who had inherited Pennsylvania from their father, agreed on where the border between Maryland and Pennsylvania should run. They also agreed to have the boundary line surveyed and marked exactly.

In the summer of 1763, Lord Baltimore and the Penns hired from England "two persons who . . . are well-skilled in astronomy, mathematicks and surveying to mark, run out, settle, fix and determine all such parts of the circle, marks, lines and boundaries" of Maryland and Pennsylvania. The "two persons," Charles Mason, who was about thirty-five, and Jeremiah Dixon, who was some five years younger, worked under England's leading astronomer at the Royal Observatory in Greenwich, England. Mason and Dixon were not only skilled astronomers and mathematicians, but they were also willing to work in the wilderness that was America.

Both men had a spirit of adventure. In order to calculate the distance between the earth and the sun, Mason and Dixon, among others, had set sail for the South Pacific in 1761 to observe the planet Venus as it passed across the face of the sun. Although Mason and Dixon made it only as far as the Cape of Good Hope on the southern tip of Africa, later scientists judged their observations to be among the most accurate of the whole project.

On August 10, 1763, Thomas Penn wrote from England that Mason and Dixon had sailed for America with their special instruments. "Mr. Mason and Mr. Dixon have taken their passages with Captain Falconar . . . and they have with them the fine Sector, two Transit Instruments, and two reflecting Telescopes."

Because Lord Baltimore and the Penns lived in England, they had appointed fourteen American Commissioners to be in charge of the survey, seven from Maryland and seven from Pennsylvania. As soon as Mason and Dixon arrived in Philadelphia on November 15, 1763, they met with the Commissioners to plan the work ahead. By the time the meetings were over, winter had set in and there was nothing for the two Englishmen to do but establish their headquarters and wait until spring to begin work.

Mason briefly mentioned the location that they had selected for

In 1763, Philadelphia is the largest city in America, seen here from the Jersey shoreline across the Delaware River.

their headquarters. "Fixed on the House of Mr. John Harland's (about 31 Miles West of Philadelphia) to bring our Instruments to," he wrote in his journal on January 8, 1764. Mr. Harland lived at the Forks of the Brandywine, where two streams, the East Branch and the West Branch, came together to form Brandywine Creek.

Mason and Dixon weren't about to take any chances transporting their valuable equipment from Philadelphia to the Forks of the Brandywine. For the two-day journey, they carefully packed their "Instruments into the wagons, except the Telescope, etc., of the Sector which was carried on the Springs (with Feather Bed under it) of a single Horse Chair."

It wasn't until April of 1764 that the Commissioners finally gave Mason and Dixon their working orders. Considering that Pontiac's Rebellion had been crushed only six months before, it may be that Mason and Dixon were relieved that they didn't have to head west into the wilderness. Instead, they were to survey and mark the boundary between Maryland and Pennsylvania that ran north and south on the Delmarva Peninsula. (The name Delmarva is a combination of DELaware, MARyland and VirginiA.)

What is now the state of Delaware was then a part of Pennsylvania known as the Three Lower Counties. Mason and Dixon were to begin their survey on the Delmarva Peninsula at a location that was called the Middle Point, the Middle Point being halfway between Cape Henlopen on the Atlantic Ocean and Chesapeake Bay. From the Middle Point, they were to run the line north until it intersected the northern boundary of the Three Lower Counties. The northern boundary line of the Three Lower Counties, which had already been surveyed, was the arc of a circle that had a twelve-mile radius, with the bell tower of the New Castle courthouse as the center of the circle.

Mason described in his journal the very large crew that he and Dixon hired after their arrival on the Delmarva Peninsula. "Engaged ax men, etc. The whole company including Steward, Tent keepers, Cooks, Chain carriers, etc. amounting to 39. Two Waggons, Eight Horses, etc."

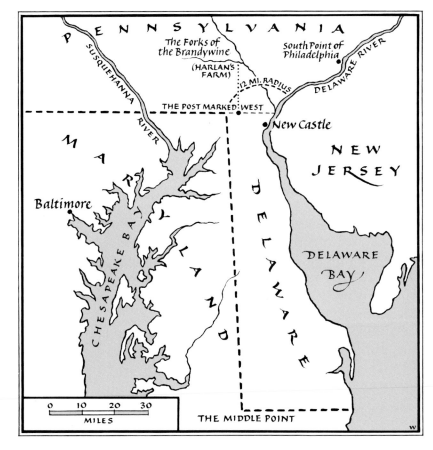

Most of the boundary line
that Mason and Dixon
are hired to survey runs
through virgin wilderness.

Because much of America in colonial times was virgin forests, ax-men were as essential to Mason and Dixon as they had been to General Braddock during the French and Indian War. Mason and Dixon's axmen had to cut down trees and undergrowth to open up an eight-or-nine-yard-wide path called a "Visto" (now known as a vista), through which telescope sightings could be made and distances measured. At the end of every mile, the crew set a wooden post in the Visto to mark the boundary line. All the land west of the posts belonged to Maryland, and Lord Baltimore, and all the land east of the posts belonged to Pennsylvania, and the Penns.

Mason, Dixon and their crew worked from dawn to dusk. "Put down the 7 Mile Post" . . . "Fixed the 44th Mile Post" . . . "Set the 74th Mile Post" were Mason's businesslike entries in his journal as the survey slowly advanced, one, two, or at best three miles a day.

It was no wonder that progress was slow. Surveying required three kinds of measurement—distances, heights and angles. Distances on level ground were measured with a 66-foot-long iron chain called a Gunter's chain that was held at either end by a chain carrier. Each chain was made up of one hundred links, with every link measuring 7.92 inches. When Mason noted in his journal that they had set a post at 48 miles 22 chains 8 links north of the Middle Point, that meant they had measured 48 miles, 485 yards, 2 feet and several inches from their starting point.

Height and angles were measured with an instrument called a transit. The transit had a compass and a telescope that allowed Mason and Dixon to take vertical and horizontal measurements. By trigonometry, they could then compute distance, height and angles over differing levels of terrain.

Eight months after they had begun, Mason and Dixon had fin-

A transit has both a telescope and a compass to assure accurate measurements.

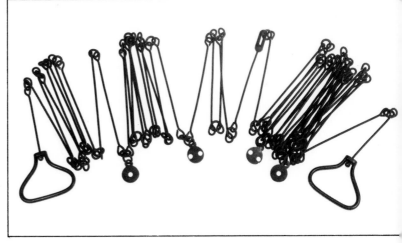

Wrought-iron chains that measure distances can be folded up and stored in a pouch for carrying.

ished surveying and setting wooden posts along the Maryland-Pennsylvania border on the Delmarva Peninsula. To make sure that their almost 82-mile-long boundary line was accurate, they resurveyed the line by observing the position of the stars and making calculations every eleven and a half miles. "Discharged all hands and left off for the winter season," Mason noted on November 26, 1764. "Returned to Mr. Harlands in the Forks of the Brandywine."

Now that they had some free time, Mason and Dixon, who were apparently fascinated by tales of frontier violence, went sightseeing. In January of 1765, they traveled to the Lancaster County jail, where the Paxton boys had murdered and scalped the band of innocent Conestoga Indians the year before. "What brought me here was my curiosity to see the place where was perpetuated last Winter the Horrid and inhuman murder of 26 Indians, Men, Women and Children, leaving none alive to tell," Mason reported in his journal. "Strange it was that the Town though as large as most Market Towns in England, never offered to oppose them . . . no honor to them!"

While in Lancaster, Mason and Dixon met former Sheriff Samuel Smith and heard first-hand about the Maryland Monster, Thomas Cresap, and his Conojacular War. Settling the border dispute between Maryland and Pennsylvania was, after all, the reason they had come to America in the first place.

"I fell in company with Mr. Samuel Smith who in the year 1736 was Sheriff of Lancaster Country," Mason wrote. "The People near the supposed Boundary Line were then at open war. About ten miles from Lancaster on the River Susquehanna one Mr. Crisep defended his house as being in Maryland, with 14 Men, which he [Sheriff Smith] surrounded with about 55. They would not surrender (but kept firing out) till the House was set on fire, and one man in the House lost his life."

Visiting Lancaster must have inspired Mason to do some more sightseeing. Two weeks later, he set out alone for New York City. On the way he had a narrow escape when he and his horse fell through the ice while crossing the frozen Delaware River. "My

Horse near being lost" was how he coolly summed up his misadventure. New York City was obviously a disappointment. "At New York" was all Mason had to say about the second-largest city in the colonies on February 17, followed by "Ditto" for both February 18 and 19.

"Met some boys just come out of a Quaker Meeting House as if the Devil had been with them," Mason noted about another mishap on his return trip. "I could by no means get my Horse by them. I gave the Horse a light blow on the Head with my whip which brought him to the ground as if shot dead. I over his Head, my hat one way wig another and whip another, fine sport for the boys." Mason must have taken quite a tumble. "Lay too—my Hip being hurt very much by the fall," he complained the next day.

Working in the Maryland-Pennsylvania wilderness might prove to be safer than traveling around the colonies after all. Mason and Dixon would soon find out. In March of 1765, they received word from the Commissioners that they were to begin their survey westward. Despite any misgivings the two men might have had, Mason's journal entry for April 5, 1765, was typically brief. "Began to run the western Line."

Mason and Dixon's headquarters at the Forks of the Brandywine was thirty-one miles west of Philadelphia. Because they had been told that the boundary line between Maryland and Pennsylvania was to start exactly fifteen miles south of "the Southernmost Point of the City of Philadelphia," they had located that spot the year before in a field "belonging to Mr. Alexander Bryan." There, at a latitude of 39 degrees, 43 minutes, 17.4 seconds north of the Equator, they had placed a "Post marked West," from which all their calculations would be made.

Once work began, Mason didn't have time to jot down much more in his journal than, "Continued the line" . . . "Continued the line" . . . "Continued the line." Mason worked as hard, if not harder, than anyone else. "To prove the Chain Carriers had made no error in the measurement," he wrote, "I took a man with me, and measured it myself." At least every seventh day was marked simply "(Sunday)", a chance for everyone to rest and relax.

A page in Mason's journal indicates that a knowledge of math is needed to calculate the Delmarva Peninsula boundary line.

Daylight

140/10/41

12 Miles

at Lat
22.51

A

B

C

N

m.b. d. lii
7.39.49
42.43.16
40.49

m. d. lii
79.52.99

m. d. lii
81.74-65

m. d. lii
81.74-25

163.68.9.08 lii
& line 81.78.31
8000

81.78.31
80
6480
78
6558.31

68.900 / 3.8612
65.900
43.900
1.900.0
0.900.0
0.900.0

3.32.1
0.17.41 E

.005

Jan'y 89.51.9

163,8612

41
20 +

7.6989700
12.5871456
10.2861156

12.214.47.57
8,0716399

M

180
17.41½

179.42.18

89.51.9
41
90.52.9

8000 / 40.000.00,5
40.000
.005

11

12.58203.04
5.1.52
12.5871456

Although Mason never described their surroundings, in 1755 a soldier had glumly observed that the wilderness was "a desolate country uninhabited by anything but wild Indians, bears, and rattlesnakes." An English traveler's account was somewhat more dramatic. "He did not know at what tread his foot might be stung by a serpent, at what moment he might meet with the formidable bear, or, if in the evening, he knew not on what limb of a tree, over his head, the murderous panther might be perched, to drop down upon him and tear him to pieces."

Accustomed as they were to the quiet English countryside, to their credit the two scientists kept going. By late fall, they had surveyed 115 miles from the "Post marked West in Mr. Bryan's field," and although they weren't finished, their goal of the Allegheny Mountains was in sight. On October 27, 1765, Mason wrote, "From here we could see the Allegany Mountains for many miles, and judge it by its appearance to be about 50 Miles distance." But winter was approaching and they had to turn back. "Packed up our Instruments and left them (not in the least damaged to our knowledge) at Captain Shelby's," Mason reported.

Captain Evan Shelby, who had served under General Braddock during the French and Indian War, was a rugged frontiersman like Thomas Cresap. Fiercely independent men such as Shelby opened up the west by ignoring Indian territorial rights and living where they pleased. To mark their property, they simply notched trees with their tomahawks, claiming "tomahawk rights" to the land.

What a relief it must have been for Mason and Dixon to be finished for the season and return to their peaceful headquarters at the Forks of the Brandywine. But if they were counting on time off, they were to be disappointed. Fifty milestones had arrived from England that the Commissioners wanted Mason and Dixon to set on the Delmarva Peninsula in place of the wooden posts. An "M" was carved on the Maryland side of each stone and a "P" on the Pennsylvania side. Every fifth mile was to be marked with a handsome crown stone that was carved with Lord Baltimore's family crest on the Maryland side and the Penn family crest on the Pennsylvania side.

"The Stones all set. Left off for the winter season," Mason wrote only two weeks later on January 1, 1766.

By the spring of 1766, the two surveyors were back at Captain Shelby's to pick up their instruments, rehire their old crew and begin work. Day after day, Mason's journal once more recorded, "Continued the line" . . . "Continued the line." They were soon deep into the Allegheny Mountains, called by some the Endless

Every fifth mile of the boundary line is marked by a crown stone that has the Penn family crest on one side and the Baltimore family crest on the other.

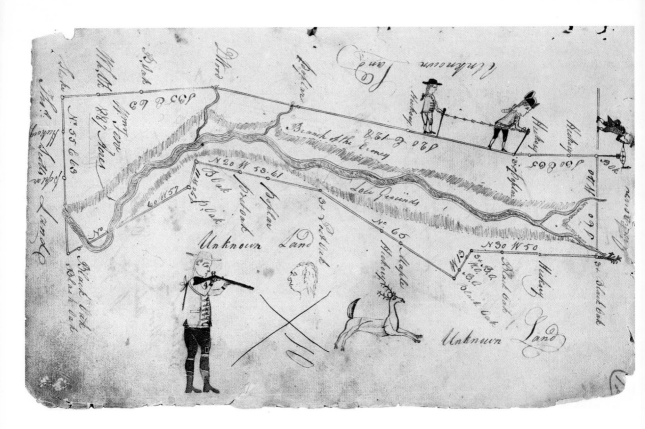

An 18th-century sketch shows a survey party at work: two chain carriers measure distances; a surveyor lines up a Black Oak tree through a telescope; a hunter kills a deer for food.

Mountains. A weary traveler wrote that the mountain range, with one steep slope following after another, was like "a choppy sea after a dreadful storm." On June 14, 1766, Mason, Dixon and their party had surveyed as far as they were allowed to go. "At present the Allegany Mountains is the boundary between the Natives and the strangers," Mason commented in his journal.

In order to control the vast North American lands acquired from France after the French and Indian War, Great Britain had issued the Proclamation of 1763. The unpopular proclamation reserved all the land beyond the crest of the Appalachian Mountains for the "Natives," or Indians, with no "strangers," or whites, permitted to settle or buy land there. The crest of the Appalachian Mountains is the eastern Continental Divide, with the rivers that flow eastward from the crest emptying into the Atlantic Ocean and the rivers that flow westward from the crest emptying into the Gulf of Mexico by way of the Ohio and Mississippi rivers.

Mason and Dixon had been instructed to survey the boundary line "as far as the land is inhabited" and that meant to the top of Savage Mountain, sometimes called Dividing Mountain because the rivers divided at its crest. In celebration of their soon-to-be-completed survey, Mason and Dixon treated themselves to a day off.

"Went to see Fort Cumberland: It is beautifully situated on a rising ground," Mason wrote. "The Fort is in bad repair; has in it at present only 10 Six Pounders [cannons]. Going to the Fort I fell into General Braddock's Road, which he cut through the Mountains to lead the Army under his command to the Westward in the year 1755, but fate; how hard: made through the desert a path, himself to pass; and never; never to return."

Viewing the road on which General Braddock had been buried was obviously a sobering experience. As Englishmen, Mason and Dixon knew only too well how the French and Indians had ambushed and destroyed the British regulars.

On June 18, 1766, Mason and Dixon reached the crest of Savage Mountain, and the end of their survey. As they made their way back toward the "Post marked West in Mr. Bryan's field," they resurveyed the line by astronomical calculations and set wooden posts in the open Visto every half-mile. By the end of September, they had finished and were safely returned to their Brandywine headquarters. But the demanding Commissioners had two more assignments for them. One was to extend their line eastward to the Delaware River and the other was to set thirty-five additional stones on the Delmarva Peninsula, as well as sixty-five stones on the Maryland-Pennsylvania boundary line heading west.

No sooner had Mason and Dixon completed both tasks than the Commissioners issued a new, and more startling, order. If the Indians gave their permission, Mason and Dixon were to run the western boundary line beyond Savage Mountain into Indian territory. For the two Englishmen to survey through the wilderness was one thing. But to survey through lands inhabited by Indians who had been waging all-out war only three years before was quite another.

CHAPTER 5

THE NATIVES
AND THE
STRANGERS

At least Mason and Dixon didn't have to decide immediately if they would continue the line into native territory. Work couldn't begin until spring and perhaps by then the Indians would have refused to give permission. Meanwhile, the two Englishmen were trying to survive the brutal winter at their Brandywine headquarters. On December 31, 1766, the thermometer registered "in the air 20° below zero," with the temperature in the tent not much better at "10° below zero." The next day was almost as bad. The "thermometer in the Air 12° below zero . . . in the Tent 9° below zero." As late as March 13 the temperature hovered around 7°.

Even with the arrival of spring, there was still no word from the Indians. On April 9, 1767, Mason wrote: "The Gentlemen Commissioners . . . had not received any positive answer from General Johnson, whether the Indians will permit us to continue the West Line or not." If anyone could reach an agreement with the Indians, Superintendent of Indian Affairs Sir William Johnson could. Johnson, who was called Warraghiyagey by the Iroquois, meaning He-Who-Does-Much, was an adopted and greatly beloved member of the Mohawk tribe.

Nevertheless, it wasn't until June 2, 1767, that Mason reported that Johnson "had made an agreement with the Indians for to let us continue the West Line." But permission was granted only if deputies from the Six Nations of the Iroquois accompanied the survey party.

The Six Nations of the Iroquois was a confederation of the Mohawk, Oneida, Onondaga, Cayuga, Seneca and Tuscarora tribes. During the French and Indian War, the Six Nations of the Iroquois had fought with the English against the Algonquian tribes, their traditional enemies, and the French, whom they detested.

Mohawks sit around their council fire in front of Sir William Johnson's New York home, where they are always welcome.

As soon as Mason and Dixon announced that they were willing to survey into Indian territory, the Commissioners forwarded a lengthy list of instructions. "As the public Peace and your own

Old Hendrick, a famous Mohawk chief, makes a notch in the tree for every enemy killed or captured.

Security may greatly depend on the good Usage and kind Treatment of these Deputies, we commit them to your particular Care," they were advised. "Be careful that they receive no Abuse or ill treatment from the Men you may employ." The subject of liquor required further instructions. "The Commissioners recommend to Messrs Mason and Dixon That the spirituous Liquors to be given to the Indians attending them, be in small quantities mixed with water and delivered to them not more than three times every day."

Like it or not, by June 15, 1767, Mason and Dixon were on their way. "Sent 7 Men with the Telescope of the Sector to Fort Cumberland. The rest of the Instruments etc. by a Waggon," Mason noted in his journal. Three weeks later, Mason and Dixon had caught up to their instruments at Fort Cumberland, where they finally met the notorious Thomas Cresap, now a wealthy land-owner. "Lodged with Colonel Crisep," Mason wrote, misspelling Cresap's name, as did almost everyone else. "He has here a most beautiful Estate." Beautiful or not, the two men didn't linger long. By the next day, they were "At the Allegeny Mountain; where we left off last Summer."

Two days later, on July 16, Mason reported their first meeting with the Indian deputies. "This day we were joined with 14 Indians, viz. Mohawks and Onondagas sent by the Six Nations to conduct us through their country, namely three Onondagas and eleven Mohawks. (With them came Mr. Hugh Crawford, Interpreter.)"

Incredibly, Mason didn't describe the new arrivals in any way, not their appearance, clothing or language. He had more to say, in fact, about their interpreter, Hugh Crawford, who had served on the western frontier during the French and Indian War. Crawford, Mason observed, had "traversed these parts for 28 years, either as an Indian Trader or Commander in his Majesty's Service."

Still not mentioning either their fourteen Indian deputies or their surroundings, Mason simply recorded his usual "Continued the line" for the next two weeks. But Laurel Hill apparently impressed him enough to rate an entry in his journal. "Laurel Hill (or rather Mountains), is a Wild of Wildes; the Laurel overgrown, the Rocks gaping to swallow up, over whose deep mouths you may step. The whole a deep melancholy appearance out of nature." This sinister sitting was where George Washington had attacked an encampment of sleeping French soldiers to launch the French and Indian War thirteen years before.

George Washington wasn't the only one to run into trouble on Laurel Hill. Mason and Dixon encountered a party of Delaware

Indians at the very same spot. "We were paid a visit by 13 Delawares; one of them a Nephew of Captain Black-Jacobs, who was killed by General Armstrong at Kittony Town," Mason wrote on August 17, 1767. "This Nephew of Black-Jacobs was the tallest Man I ever saw."

These particular Delaware Indians were what Mason and Dixon *didn't* want to meet. Some ten years earlier, Captain Black-Jacobs and a Delaware war party had massacred or captured all the families in a settlement near Bedford, Pennsylvania. In revenge, Colonel John Armstrong and 300 volunteers had burned down the Delaware camp at Kittanning and killed forty Indians, including Captain Black-Jacobs. Now here was Captain Black-Jacobs' nephew himself!

Remarkably, their meeting with the thirteen Delawares passed without incident . . . except that two of Mason and Dixon's Indian deputies departed immediately afterwards. "Mr. John Green, one of the Chiefs of the Mohawk Nation, and his Nephew left us, in order to return to their own Country," Mason noted. Mohawks, whose name meant "man-eater," were known for their bravery, but like the Half-King and his braves at Fort Necessity, Mr. John Green and his nephew weren't foolhardy. Knowing that they were deep in enemy territory and seriously outnumbered, the two Mohawks bid their farewells and departed.

If Mason and Dixon were also tempted to return to "their own country," Mason didn't mention it. The only evidence of the mounting tension was that for the first time, Mason and Dixon had their crew work right on through the following Sunday. Nevertheless, by the middle of September 1767, as the survey party traveled ever westward, the Indian deputies became more and more restless. "Here two of the Mohawks made an objection against our passing the [Cheat] River, but a Council being call'd, the Chiefs determin'd we should pass," Mason wrote.

Only two weeks later, on the banks of the Monongahela River, Mason reported a full-blown rebellion. "Twenty-six of our Men left us: they would not pass the [Monongahela] River for fear of the Shawanes and Delaware Indians." A number of the deserters were members of the survey crew, local men who had seen first-hand what Delaware and Shawnee war parties were capable of.

Those deserters may have known what lay ahead. Almost as soon as Mason, Dixon and the remaining members of their party crossed the Monongahela River, a family of Delawares made their appearance. "About two miles west of Monaungahela we were paid a visit by Catfish, his Nephew, and Squaw (or wife)," Mason related. "They were very well dressed nearly like Europeans; and he (Catfish) being a chief of the Delaware Nation, our Chief held a Council and made a Speech (and presented him with some strings of Wampom) to him; in which they acquainted them of our business there."

Although there were only three Delawares, the fact that a Council was held and strings of wampum exchanged indicated that Catfish was a very important chief indeed. And he was. A village, built on the site of Chief Catfish's encampment in Pennsylvania, was called Catfish Camp until 1781 when the name was changed to Washington. Apparently, Chief Catfish realized that the survey party was on a peaceful mission, as Mason concluded his journal entry by noting that Catfish "seemed to be very well satisfied, and promised to send the strings of Wampom to his Town."

Even the Commissioners couldn't have blamed Mason and Dixon if they had stopped then and there. But they had surveyed over 225 miles, and although they were shorthanded, they weren't about to give up. Nevertheless, because they had to send back to Fort Cumberland to replace the workers who had quit, it was five days before they were on their way again.

Six miles later, an Indian war party emerged from the forests. To everyone's relief, it was a band of friendly Senecas on their way south to wage war. "Eight warriors of the Seneca Nation fell in with us, in their way to the Southward going against the Cherokees," Mason explained. "They are one of the Six Nations, which made the Indians with us, very glad to see them. They were equipped with Blankets and Kettles, Tomahawks Guns and Bows and Arrows; they staid two days with us, got a small supply of Powder and paint: when their Captain ordered to march."

For those two days, at least, the presence of a well-armed Seneca war party must have reassured the survey crew. Not that their Indian deputies weren't well-armed themselves. The fact that they were able to supply the Senecas with gunpowder and war paint indicated that they, too, were prepared for combat.

On October 9, 1767, shortly after the Senecas had left, Mason reported that the survey party "Crossed a War Path," just before reaching Dunkard Creek. "This Creek takes its name from a small town settled by the Dunchards," was Mason's comment about a religious community of Germans who had founded the Dunkard Church. "The town was burnt, and most of the Inhabitants killed by the Indians in 1755."

Warpaths were no joking matter. About a foot wide and sometimes as much as six inches deep, a warpath was a hidden trail in the forest used by war parties to approach an enemy camp secretly. The combination of a warpath and the reminder of the massacre that had wiped out the entire Dunkard settlement alarmed everyone, especially the Indian deputies, who refused to continue. "This day the Chief of the Indians which joined us on the 16th of July informed us that the above mentioned War Path was the extent of his commission from the Chiefs of the Six Nations that he should go with us, with the Line: and that he would not proceed one step farther Westward," Mason wrote.

By the next day a worried Mason was commenting: "The Indians with us still persisting that they will not go any farther Westward with the Line." That settled it. Without their Iroquois escort, Mason and Dixon had to call a halt to the survey at "233 miles 17 chains 48 Links from the Post Marked West in Mr. Bryan's field." Unknown to Mason and Dixon, they had actually surveyed some thirty miles of the border that separated Pennsylvania and Virginia, stopping at Brown's Hill near present-day Morgantown, West Virginia. (West Virginia didn't become a state until 1863.)

Mason, Dixon, their crew and what few Indians were left immediately began the long trek back east, resurveying the line the

Mason's journal records that the Iroquois deputies are increasingly concerned as the survey party travels deeper into "Native" territory.

1767
Sept:

☿ — 9   Continued the Line.
At 116·32 { Cross'd McColloch's Creek :
running Northerly.

♃ — 10   Continued the Line.
At 217·13 cross'd ye above Creek a 2 time
this is at ye foot of Laurel Hill on ye West side.
At 217·51 Cross'd the the above Creek a 3 time.

♀ — 11   Continued the Line.
At 218·31 { Cross'd the above mention'd Creek a 4 time.
running South^{ly}:

♄ — 12   Continued the Line.
At 219·22·25 The East Bank of the River
Cheat. and at 219·34·50 The West Bank of
the said River. ———— We cross'd the River
Obliquely, but at Right Angles it is about Ten
chains in breadth. having very level smooth bottom.
The water at present very low, and is con
tain'd in some places, where it runs; in about 20 yards wide
and about two feet deep.
Here, two of the Mohocks made an objection against our
passing the River, but a council being call'd, the chiefs
⊙ — 13   determin'd we should pass.

☽ — 14   Continued the Line.
♂ — 15   Continued the Line.
☿ — 16   Continued the Line.
At { 221·00 } Cross'd a small Runs, now nearly
{ 222·09 } dry. ————

whole way. Although 132 milestones marked the eastern end of the boundary line, there was no way to transport the heavy stones over the mountains to mark the western end. In place of stones, Mason and Dixon had their men pile rocks and mounds of earth around wooden posts to serve as mile markers.

Although danger from the Indians lessened the farther east the survey party traveled, the terrible cold and mountain snows made the next one hundred miles almost impassable. Mason's journal entries for November noted: "Snow" . . . "Snow 12 or 14 inches deep" . . . "The weather so bad our Hands would not proceed."

It wasn't until December of 1767 that Mason and Dixon finally reached Philadelphia, their survey completed. All they had left to do was meet with the Commissioners and be formally discharged. But when they attended what should have been their last meeting, the Commissioners gave them still another assignment. "The Gentlemen Commissioners did not choose to give us a discharge in writing," Mason fretted. "Received Instructions to Draw a Map or Plan of the Lines."

It was another eight months before Mason could finally write: "Two Hundred Copies of the Plans of the Lines [were] printed off." Ten days later, at their last meeting with the Commissioners, Mason noted, "Our accounts were settled, and the whole work of our part . . . was entirely finished." On September 11, 1768, Mason penned his final journal entry: "At 11h 30m A.M. went on Board the Halifax Packet Boat for Falmouth. Thus ends my restless progress in America.

C. Mason"

Charles Mason and Jeremiah Dixon had survived demanding Commissioners, accidents, hostile Indians, snow-covered mountains, swollen rivers and wild animals. Although their American adventure had ended in September of 1768, they didn't submit their final bill to Lord Baltimore and the Penns until after they had returned to England in November. "For our passage to America and passage hence to England (£84). Total, £3516.19.00" (At that time, an English country squire could live comfortably on £300 or £400 a year.)

It was a modest ending for a brilliant scientific achievement. Later surveys in 1849 and 1901-1903, which were made with more sophisticated equipment than were available to Mason and Dixon, revealed only a slight margin of error. The two English scientists had surveyed and marked the boundary line between Maryland and Pennsylvania once and for all.

As for Mason's use of the expression "restless progress," perhaps it was deliberate. During the five years that Mason and Dixon had lived and worked in North America, it would have been hard for them not to notice that the colonies, too, were experiencing "restless progress." After winning the French and Indian War in 1763, England had not only slapped heavy taxes and duties on the colonies to help pay for that war, but had also dictated where Americans could or could not live. And the colonials didn't like these new restrictions one bit. They had flexed their muscles during the war years and found them strong. Objections and protests mounted. The course for conflict was set and there would be no turning back.

It takes Mason and Dixon many months to complete a map of the boundary line between Maryland and Pennsylvania, a section of which is reproduced here.

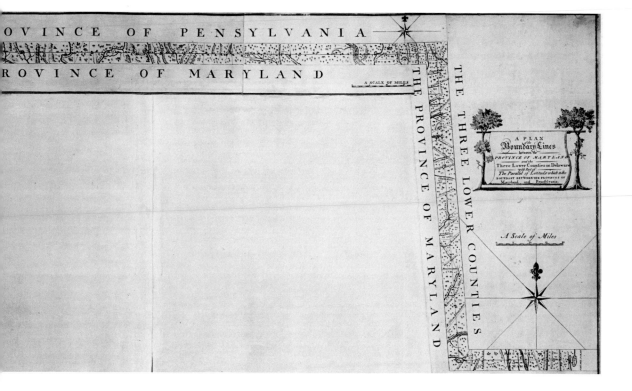

CHAPTER 6

"OUR ARMY WAS SOMETHING BROKE"

Charles Mason and Jeremiah Dixon found a home away from home at the Forks of the Brandywine in Pennsylvania, where two meandering streams, the East Branch and the West Branch, came together to form Brandywine Creek. It must have been with a sense of pleasure that Mason penned in his journal: "Returned to the Forks of the Brandywine" . . . "At Brandywine" . . . "Returned to Brandywine."

From the Forks, Brandywine Creek flowed south across Mason and Dixon's line into the Three Lower Counties, and from there into the Delaware River. In 1776, the Three Lower Counties broke away from Pennsylvania to become the independent state of Delaware, the only state to have an arc of a circle as one of its borders. It was a year after that, in 1777, that the fires of the American Revolution ignited along Pennsylvania's peaceful Brandywine Creek, just a few miles north of Mason and Dixon's line.

The Revolution had begun at Lexington and Concord on April

Brandywine Creek, which winds through Pennsylvania's lovely Brandywine Valley, is the setting for a Revolutionary War battle.

19, 1775, with "the shot heard 'round the world," as the thirteen colonies began an eight-year struggle to win their freedom from England. In the summer of 1777, after a string of British victories, the commander in chief of the British Army, General William Howe, made plans to split the United States in two by invading Pennsylvania and capturing the capital of Philadelphia. Howe believed that Philadelphia was a hotbed of Tories loyal to the king who were only waiting to be liberated by the British forces.

While General Howe was making plans, the commander in chief of the American forces, General George Washington, was camped with his army north of Philadelphia. Washington knew that General Howe was about to launch a campaign but he didn't know where. As he waited out his "truly delicate and perplexing" situation, a red-haired, nineteen-year-old Frenchman, the Marquis de Lafayette, appeared at camp to offer Washington his services. "The moment I heard of America, I loved her," Lafayette announced. "The moment I knew she was fighting for freedom, I burned with a desire of bleeding for her." At their very first meeting, Washington and Lafayette struck up an immediate and lifelong friendship.

It wasn't until July 31, 1777, that Washington learned that Howe with 13,000 British regulars and 5,000 professional German soldiers, called Hessians, had boarded transport ships off the Jersey coast and sailed south. Realizing that Howe's destination must be Philadelphia, Washington immediately broke camp and headed for the capital. Because Philadelphia *was* a hotbed of Tories, Washington marched his 10,000 men through the city in a show of strength. To give their shabby and mismatched uniforms a look of unity, the troops were ordered to wear a sprig of green leaves in their hats. Riding through Philadelphia beside Washington, Lafayette observed: "Their heads covered with green branches and marching to the sound of drums and fifes, these soldiers, in spite of their state of nudity, offered an agreeable spectacle to the eyes of all citizens."

Washington needn't have hurried. Because Howe had heard

This painting, dated 1777, is the only known portrait of British General William Howe.

that the Delaware River was both hazardous to navigation and heavily defended, he decided to approach Philadelphia by sailing all the way around the Delmarva Peninsula and up Chesapeake Bay, a difficult voyage that took over a month. It wasn't until September 10 that the British Army assembled under General Howe in the village of Kennett Square, Pennsylvania.

By now, Washington's forces, which had been increased to 13,000 men, were positioned on Brandywine Creek, some twenty-five miles southwest of Philadelphia. Brandywine Creek, which flowed through the Brandywine Valley between steep hills, could be crossed on foot at only five shallow locations, called fords. Because the road that the British Army would have to take from Kennett Square to Philadelphia crossed Brandywine Creek at Chad's Ford, only two miles north of Mason and Dixon's line, Washington stationed the main body of his men on the east bank of Chad's Ford. To protect the other four fords, Washington posted divisions all along the eastern hills overlooking Brandywine Creek.

On the morning of September 11, 1777, General Wilhelm von Knyphausen marched his British and Hessian troops from Kennett Square to the west bank of Chad's Ford, where they took up their position. By 10:30 A.M., the two armies faced each other across Brandywine Creek, and although some artillery fire was exchanged, neither side did any real damage to the other.

What followed would have been a comedy of errors if so many lives hadn't been at stake. Unknown to Washington, the British plan was for Knyphausen, who commanded only about 5,000 men, to trick the Americans into thinking that the entire British force was about to make a frontal attack across Chad's Ford. Meanwhile, General Howe and Lord Charles Cornwallis, at the head of 13,000 men, were marching up Great Valley Road that ran west of Brandywine Creek and parallel to it. Hidden from American forces by wooded hills, the British planned to cross the West Branch and the East Branch one mile *above* the Forks of the Brandywine and come around behind Washington's right flank in a surprise attack. (The British had successfully used the same tactics the year before on Long Island.)

But this time the British troops had been spotted. About 11 A.M. Washington was informed that the enemy had been sighted marching up Great Valley Road and was about to cross at Trimble's Ford on the West Branch, above the Forks of the Brandywine. Washington, who had earlier been told (incorrectly) that there was no road in that area and no fords for many miles above the Forks, was astonished. "You will send an intelligent, sensible officer immediately with a party to find out the truth," Washington commanded Colonel Theodorick Bland. Only a short time later, Bland notified Washington that he himself had seen the enemy advancing on "the valley road."

A clever British maneuver fools the American military.

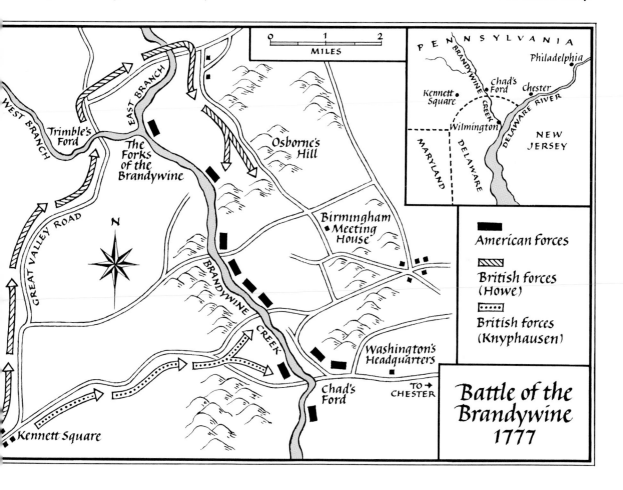

American forces

British forces (Howe)

British forces (Knyphausen)

Battle of the Brandywine 1777

In response, Washington directed two divisions to cross Brandywine Creek to halt the British advance. But almost as soon as he had issued the order, a dispatch arrived from General John Sullivan stating that earlier "information must be wrong." There was no enemy force marching up Great Valley Road. Incredibly, despite all reports to the contrary, Washington pulled back his two divisions and again sat tight to await a frontal attack by Knyphausen across Chad's Ford.

Time passed and Knyphausen made no move. And then, about 2 P.M., an excited local farmer named Thomas Cheyney arrived at Washington's headquarters to report that British troops had crossed both the West Branch and the East Branch and were approaching Washington's lines from the rear. When Washington and his aides challenged his word, Farmer Cheyney lost his temper. "You're mistaken, General. My life for it you're mistaken," he insisted. "Put me under guard till you can find out it's so!"

Moments later, a courier arrived with a message from General Sullivan, settling the argument. The enemy had indeed marched behind the right flank of Washington's troops and taken a position on Obsorne's Hill. Washington immediately sent three divisions to the rear, keeping some units at Chad's Ford in case of an attack by Knyphausen. When the three divisions reached the rear, they took a stand near Birmingham Meeting House on a hill that was something over a mile across a valley from the British troops on Osborne's Hill. They didn't have long to wait. Shortly after 4 P.M., the British and Hessian soldiers, in dress uniform, with their bayonets "shining like silver," paraded down Osborne's Hill. As they marched in perfect formation across the valley, the Americans opened fire and the battle was on.

Back at Chad's Ford, Washington, who was still awaiting a frontal attack from Knyphausen, heard "a sudden burst of cannon from the northwestward." Although he was certain that the fighting had started, it was another half hour before he ordered the main strength of his army to the rear. Lafayette had already ridden to the scene of the battle, and now Washington prepared to go, too. But none of his staff knew how to get there. A bystander, an

The American army fights
valiantly at Brandywine
against superior
British forces.

elderly farmer named Joseph Brown, was asked to lead the general
to Birmingham Meeting House, but he refused. Threatening
Brown with his sword, one of Washington's aides ordered the
surly old farmer to show them the way or else! Brown, with an
instant change of heart, mounted a horse and led the little party
across the countryside, with Washington urging him on the whole
way, *"Push along, old man—Push along, old man."*

By the time Washington arrived at Birmingham Meeting
House, the fighting was heavy. Five times the Americans were
pushed back and five times they regained their position. For an
hour and forty minutes, the two armies fought "almost Muzzle to
Muzzle," with an American officer declaring that "cannon balls
flew thick and many and small arms roared like the rolling of a
drum." Although Washington and Lafayette rode among the men
to rally them, the British forces broke through the American line
and the order to withdraw was given.

Back at Chad's Ford, Knyphausen had also heard the cannonading from the rear that was his signal to attack. Under steady American fire, his men forded Brandywine Creek. A Hessian officer described the crossing: "The water took us up to our breasts and was much stained with blood." One of Cornwallis's brigades, which had gotten lost in the battle to the rear, now came stumbling out of the woods behind the American line. With Knyphausen's men attacking from the front and a British brigade suddenly appearing to their rear, the American effort at Chad's Ford collapsed. A Jersey soldier wrote that because "our army was something broke, it was necessary to leave the field of action."

Now thousands of American soldiers retreated in total confusion toward Chester, twelve miles away. Although he was wounded, Lafayette stationed himself at the Chester Creek bridge to try to restore order. Even so, it was after midnight before the

Lafayette is wounded during his first American battle.

chaos was brought under control and Lafayette's leg wound could be attended to. "Treat him as if he were my son, for I love him as if he were," Washington ordered.

Records from the Battle of the Brandywine are vague. About 200 Americans were killed, maybe 700 to 800 were wounded, with "near 400" taken prisoner. In the British Army 89 were killed, 488 wounded and 6 missing. Despite his errors and hesitations, Washington wasn't downhearted and neither were his men. They had fought well and they knew it. Although Philadelphia fell to the British as a result of the Battle of the Brandywine, Congress simply moved to York, Pennsylvania, and set up business there.

As for Washington, once again he had waged war on the battle-ground that was Mason and Dixon's line. And once again he had been defeated. But the Battle of the Brandywine on September 11, 1777, was only a defeat and not a disaster. The American Army may have been "something broke," but it wasn't destroyed and Washington had learned that keeping the army together was more important than winning any one battle or holding on to a certain piece of land. The British didn't call Washington the Old Fox for nothing. Like a sly old fox, Washington always managed to escape at the last minute. "We fight, get beat, rise, and fight again," bragged one of his generals.

The Battle of the Brandywine also marked a turning point in the American Revolution. When the war had begun, soldiers had resented having to serve under an officer from another village. But at Brandywine, a Jerseyman had been in command of detachments from Virginia, a Pennsylvania officer had held his position with Jersey troops, and an officer from Rhode Island had led a Virginia division. For the first time, Washington had commanded a truly American army.

The fires of war that had ignited along Mason and Dixon's line in the Brandywine Valley had been stamped out without serious damage to America's struggle for freedom. With a new sense of unity, the Continental Army had survived to fight again another day, and be victorious in the end.

𝕍

THE WHISKEY BOYS AND THE WATERMELON ARMY

The end of the American Revolution didn't mean the end of fighting, or the end of George Washington's military career either. In the 1790s, Mason and Dixon's line again became the scene of violence, this time between an angry mob of western Pennsylvania farmers and the new federal government of the United States.

Actually, those hotheaded westerners had been causing trouble for years. Although King George III had formally approved Mason and Dixon's survey in 1769, during the 1770s, Pennsylvanians and Virginians had begun quarreling over the location of their mutual borderline. It wasn't until 1780 that Pennsylvania and Virginia agreed on where that borderline should be and hired surveyors to begin work just west of Dunkard's Creek, where Mason and Dixon had left off. But armed Virginia settlers prevented the survey from being completed. Finally, in November of 1782, a temporary line was run between Pennsylvania and Virginia. "We have

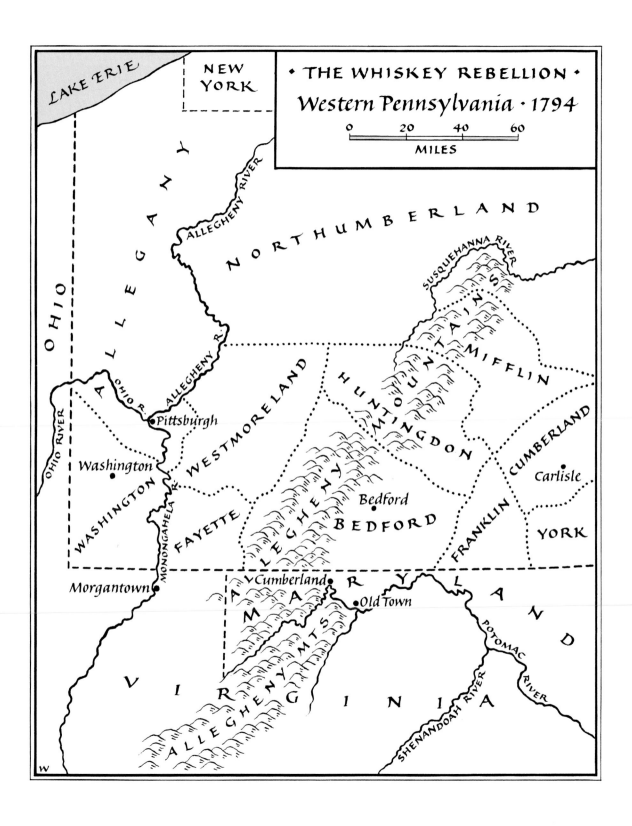

LAKE ERIE

NEW YORK

• THE WHISKEY REBELLION •
Western Pennsylvania · 1794

0   20   40   60
MILES

ALLEGANY

ALLEGHENY RIVER

NORTHUMBERLAND

SUSQUEHANNA RIVER

MOUNTAINS

MIFFLIN

OHIO

ALLEGHENY R.

ALLEGHENY R.

Pittsburgh

WESTMORELAND

HUNTINGDON

CUMBERLAND

OHIO RIVER

OHIO R.

Washington

WASHINGTON

MONONGAHELA R.

FAYETTE

ALLEGHENY

Bedford

BEDFORD

FRANKLIN

Carlisle

YORK

Morgantown

MARYLAND

Cumberland

Old Town

POTOMAC RIVER

VIRGINIA

ALLEGHENY MTS

SHENANDOAH RIVER

RIVER

W

extended Dixon's and Mason's line 23 miles to a small poplar [tree] on the forks of Fish Creek," read the report.

Andrew Ellicott was one of the surveyors who helped complete the permanent line three years later. In May of 1785, Ellicott visited the indomitable Thomas Cresap in Old Town. "This evening I spent with the celebrated Col. Cresap," Ellicott wrote. "He lost his eyesight about 18 months past, but his other faculties are yet unimpaired, his sense strong and manly, and his ideas flow with ease."

The following year, Mason and Dixon's line that separated Pennsylvania and Virginia was run sixty-two miles due north. Although extension of Mason and Dixon's line both west and north settled the conflict between Pennsylvania and Virginia once and for all, in 1791, an even more serious conflict flared up along that border. To the dismay of western farmers, Congress passed a tax on whiskey, called an excise tax because it taxed a home-grown product consumed in this country. Alexander Hamilton, who had first served under General George Washington at the Battle of the Brandywine, now served as President Washington's secretary of the treasury. Although Hamilton had proposed the tax as a means of paying off the national debt, others in government predicted disaster. "War and bloodshed [are] the most likely consequence of all this," protested one senator.

He was right. The farmers and settlers in the four western Pennsylvania counties of Washington, Westmoreland, Fayette and Allegeny were bold, headstrong people who had bitter memories of excise taxes in Scotland and northern Ireland. We fought the Revolution to be rid of unjust taxation. Besides, whiskey was their lifeblood! Almost every farmer in the area either had his whiskey distilled from grain at a local still or distilled it himself. Although the average farmer didn't see $20 in cash during a year, the excise tax was to be paid in cash. Furthermore, if the tax wasn't paid, the farmer had to travel three hundred miles to the nation's capital in Philadelphia to stand trial.

With a gallon jug of whiskey worth a quarter in every local

store, whiskey was as good as gold in those four counties bounded by Mason and Dixon's line on the south and west and the Allegheny Mountains on the east. Because Spain controlled western trade on the Mississippi River, farmers had to sell their products in the east, which meant transporting goods over the Allegheny Mountains by packhorse. With one packhorse able to carry either four bushels of grain or twenty-four bushels of grain in the form of two kegs of whiskey, it wasn't difficult to figure out which product brought the highest profit.

Nothing much had changed on the frontier over the years. Arguments were still settled with violence instead of words. By the summer of 1794, resentment in the four Pennsylvania counties had reached a breaking point. Tax collectors had been tarred and feathered, whipped, robbed, had their hair cut off and their horses stolen. On July 15, 1794, the violence boiled over when a United States marshal, who was delivering arrest notices, was confronted

The value of whiskey doubles by the time packhorse trains cross the Allegheny Mountains and arrive at eastern markets.

by thirty or forty men armed with guns and pitchforks. Although the marshal escaped, his companion, John Neville, wasn't so lucky.

Neville was a wealthy local landowner who had infuriated his neighbors by becoming a federal tax inspector. Only hours after the incident, a mob of more than fifty people surrounded his handsome mansion near Pittsburgh. By dawn the next day, the mob had increased to 500. With Neville, his family, loyal servants and six militiamen defending the house, the siege soon turned into open warfare. At least one rioter was killed, a number of soldiers and rioters were wounded, and although Neville escaped, his house and all its outbuildings were burned.

Relishing their new sense of power, the mob's leaders began to bully the local people. "If you do not come forward now and support us," they warned, "you shall be treated in the same or worse manner." On July 26, the so-called Whiskey Boys robbed the mail and expelled from Pittsburgh anyone who had written letters criticizing the attack on Neville. Gathering momentum, the Whiskey Boys held mock trials, brutalized tax collectors and destroyed the stills of anyone who paid the excise tax. There was even talk of the four counties leaving the Union and forming an independent state. A local lawyer described the whole region as "one inflammable mass."

On July 30, over 5,000 citizens gathered outside Pittsburgh on Braddock's Field where General Braddock had met his fate forty years before. There the people practiced target shooting and listened to fiery speeches, while men with faces smeared with war paint ran through the crowds shouting, "Death to the traitors!" David Bradford, an ambitious lawyer from the town of Washington (formerly Catfish Camp), had already emerged as the mob's ringleader. Picturing himself as a frontier George Washington, Bradford, who assumed the rank of Major-General, rode around Braddock's Field "mounted on a superb horse . . . with plumes floating in the air and sword drawn." At nightfall, the 5,000 rioters marched on Pittsburgh. Although they threatened to set fire to the town, in the end, all they burned was a tax collector's barn.

As reports filtered back to Philadelphia, a worried President Washington asked his Cabinet for advice. Secretary of the Treasury Hamilton was all for calling up the militia and crushing the rebellion by force. Secretary of State Edmund Randolph disagreed. Using force, he said, "would heap curses upon the Government. The strength of the government is in the affection of the people."

Washington's thinking lay somewhere between the two. On the one hand, he disliked the idea of the militia taking up arms against their fellow countrymen. On the other hand, he knew that federal laws had to be obeyed or the new nation couldn't survive. If "a minority, a small one too, is to dictate to the majority, there is an end put, at one stroke, to republican government," he declared.

In the interest of keeping the peace, Washington appointed commissioners to try to talk some sense into the rebels. As a backup, he also sent out an order on September 9, 1794, for 13,000 militia, volunteers and draftees from Pennsylvania, Maryland, New Jersey and Virginia to begin assembling.

Washington's peace commissioners returned from the western counties on September 24 to announce that the Whiskey Boys had refused to cooperate in any way. Furthermore, the rebellion was spreading into central Pennsylvania, Maryland, Virginia and Kentucky. "The whole cry was war" was their pessimistic report.

An angry mob escorts a tarred and feathered tax collector out of town on a rail.

In a contemporary cartoon, the Whiskey Boys gleefully prepare to "tar and feather the rascal."

The very next day, with "the deepest regret," Washington ordered the militia to rendezvous in the two Pennsylvania towns of Carlisle and Bedford. From there they would march over the Allegheny Mountains to "bring those people to a proper sense of their duty." Washington himself would review the troops to decide if he should personally lead the army as commander in chief.

On September 30, Washington, his private secretary and Alexander Hamilton left Philadelphia by carriage. In the thirty years since Mason and Dixon had struggled through the Maryland-Pennsylvania wilderness, a few roads had been built, but they weren't much more than dirt ruts, pockmarked with tree stumps. Already slowed by the bad roads, Washington's party was further held up by the troops heading for their staging areas.

Washington was discouraged by his first glimpse of the assembled army at Carlisle. The troops had recently been dubbed the Watermelon Army because of their military failures against the Indians in the west. "Brothers, you must not think to frighten us with fine arranged lists of infantry, cavalry, and artillery composed of your watermelon armies from the Jersey shores," advised fictitious Captain Whiskey in a humorous essay that few in the military found amusing. Amusing or not, the army was living up to its name. Soldiers had already shot and killed two civilians in separate incidents, drunkenness and gambling were commonplace and discipline was nonexistent.

Washington became even more discouraged when two representatives of the Whiskey Boys arrived in Carlisle to tell him that the rebels were not only opposed to the excise law, "but to *all* law, and Government; and to the Officers of Government." Furthermore, the rebels didn't believe that the troops would actually march against them. Washington quickly set the two men straight. If the rebels gave up peacefully, there would be no bloodshed, but if they continued to cause trouble, "the government could, and would enforce obedience to the laws."

The sad state of the army at Carlisle convinced Washington that he should lead the troops and he made plans for his trip. At least whiskey wouldn't be a problem. Washington's practical secretary noted: "As the President will be going, if he proceeds, into the Country of Whiskey he proposed to make use of that liquor for his drink."

On October 12, Washington left Carlisle and headed west, crossing Mason and Dixon's line into Maryland and arriving in Old Town four days later. It must have seemed strange not to have visited with his old friend of many years' standing, but Thomas Cresap had died several years before at the age of ninety-six. Apparently the roads hadn't improved much since Washington had first lodged with Colonel Cresap almost fifty years before. "This distance from the extreme badness of the Road, more than half of it being very hilly, and great part of it Stoney, was a severe days Journey for the Carriage horses," Washington grumbled.

From Old Town, Washington drove to Cumberland, Maryland, another familiar setting from his youth. But instead of limping into Fort Cumberland as a green and inexperienced colonial officer after a disastrous defeat, President Washington rode in as the idolized commander in chief of the armed forces of the United States. By 1794, George Washington had already become a mythic figure, and his appearance had a calming effect on the men. One Pennsylvania soldier described him as "THE MAN OF THE PEOPLE," while another wrote that the soldiers showed him "the affectionate regard that would have been to an honored Parent."

Washington noted in his diary: "Remained at Cumberland, in order to acquire a true knowledge of the strength—condition—&ca. of the Troops; and to see how they were provided." After three days, he announced that he was satisfied that the army could march without him. But before returning to Philadelphia, he appointed Alexander Hamilton to be in charge of the troops, a curious choice considering that Hamilton, as the author of the excise tax, was detested by the Whiskey Boys.

"We will defeat the first army that comes over the mountains, and take their arms and baggage," the Whiskey Boys' leader, David Bradford, had earlier bragged. But word of the President's impressive journey across Pennsylvania had reached the rebels and when they heard that 12,950 men were marching over the Allegheny Mountains, they knew their cause was lost. It was. A Pennsylvania militiaman reported that when the army appeared, "The country trembled about us." Even David Bradford fled town before the army arrived, never to return.

With orders "to scour the country [and] seize the whiskey boys," the troops closed illegal stills, made mass arrests and placed 200 rebels under guard, all without firing a shot. By November 17, 1794, Alexander Hamilton sent word to Washington that the army was ready to leave for home. A general pardon was issued on November 29 for all but a handful of leaders who were marched through Philadelphia under guard. One Philadelphian noted that the rioters "wore the appearance of wretchedness."

Only two rebels were found guilty of treason, both of whom were pardoned the following year.

A triumphant Washington boasted that his "army of the Constitution" had brought the rebels to "a *perfect* sense of their misconduct without spilling a drop of blood." Washington deserved to boast. Mason and Dixon's line had once again been a battleground. This time the violence had been triggered by rebellious farmers refusing to obey a federal law. But the new President of the new democracy had acted decisively. In its first test of power, the federal government had upheld the right of Congress to pass laws and the right of the President to enforce those laws by military means. And George Washington, as commander in chief of the armed forces, had come full circle, ending forty-two years of military service in the same western border country where it had begun.

As the only President to wear a uniform while in office, George Washington reviews the troops at Fort Cumberland.

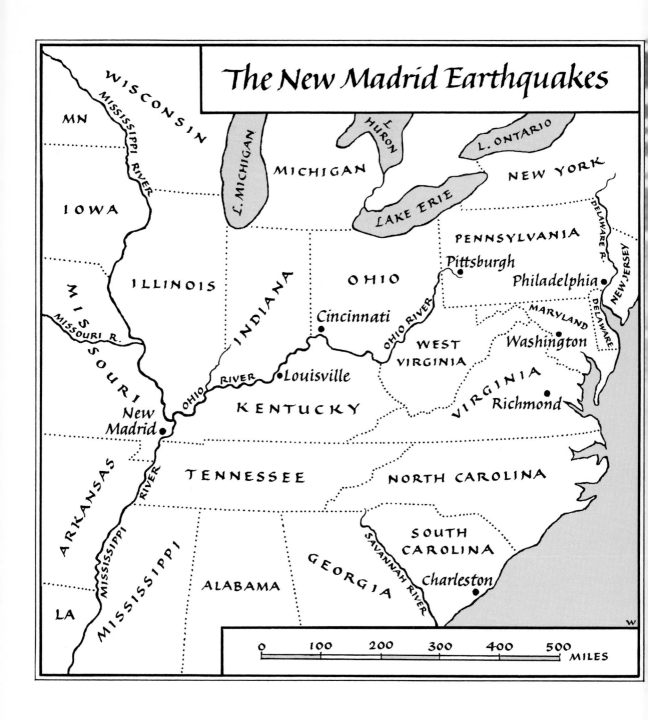

The New Madrid Earthquakes

MN

WISCONSIN

MISSISSIPPI RIVER

IOWA

ILLINOIS

MISSOURI

MISSOURI R.

L. MICHIGAN

MICHIGAN

L. HURON

LAKE ERIE

L. ONTARIO

NEW YORK

PENNSYLVANIA

Pittsburgh

Philadelphia

DELAWARE R.

NEW JERSEY

INDIANA

OHIO

Cincinnati

OHIO RIVER

WEST VIRGINIA

MARYLAND

Washington

DELAWARE

OHIO RIVER

Louisville

KENTUCKY

VIRGINIA

Richmond

New Madrid

ARKANSAS

MISSISSIPPI RIVER

TENNESSEE

NORTH CAROLINA

MISSISSIPPI

ALABAMA

GEORGIA

SAVANNAH RIVER

SOUTH CAROLINA

Charleston

LA

W

0   100   200   300   400   500
MILES

CHAPTER 8

THAT
ASTONISHING
YEAR

In 1767 Charles Mason had looked into the future. "The West Line that divides the Province of Maryland and Pennsylvania if Extended would fall on the Ohio [River], about the mouth of Fishing Creek," he had written concerning the line that by the 1770s would be known as Mason and Dixon's line. "From here a West Course would pass through the southern part of the Illinois [Territory]."

Because of America's constant urge to move ever westward, Charles Mason's prediction soon came to pass. By the early 1800s, Mason and Dixon's line had been extended some 980 miles as it traced the course of the Ohio River, from its headwaters in Pennsylvania to its junction with the Mississippi River. (The shortest route to the Ohio River was the country's earliest national road, which for its first sixty miles followed the old trail that Thomas Cresap and Nemacolin had blazed back in 1751.)

Charles Mason predicts that the boundary line that he and Dixon are surveying will one day be extended.

With a 1795 treaty with Spain opening the Mississippi River to American trade, and the purchase of the Louisiana Territory in 1803 that more than doubled the size of the United States, restless Americans traveled by flatboat and raft down the winding Ohio River to settle in the rich Ohio Valley. An English visitor remarked: "Good land, dog-cheap everywhere, and for nothing, if you will go for it, gives as much elbow room to every man as he chooses to take."

Settlements sprang up all along the Ohio River, some no more than isolated log cabins, others like Cincinnati, Ohio, and Louisville, Kentucky, good-sized towns. No matter how humbly, or how well, people lived in the Ohio and Mississippi valleys during those frontier times, none of them would ever forget *Annus Mirabilis,* that astonishing year of 1811, when nature itself turned topsy-turvy.

Although squirrels are not migrating animals, in the spring of 1811, thousands of squirrels drowned trying to cross the wide Ohio River on their way south. During that same spring, terrible flooding on the Ohio River caused the planting of crops to be delayed for weeks. Only a few months later, a Kentucky newspaper reported that "during the summer months the heat was, in many places, the most intense that was ever known," with drought destroying many of the crops that had finally been planted.

In the fall of 1811, the sky was ablaze with one of the most spectacular comets of all time, the great Comet of 1811. The head of the comet was larger than the sun, over one million miles in diameter, while its tail was more than 100 million miles long and 14 million miles wide. Along the Ohio and Mississippi rivers, the Comet of 1811 was at its brightest during September and October. Stretching halfway across the sky, its nightly appearance awed settlers and Indians alike.

Superstitious people used to believe that comets were omens of disaster and perhaps this time they were right. On December 16, 1811, the Ohio and Mississippi valleys were torn asunder by one of the great earthquakes in the history of the world. The epicenter

of the quake was in uninhabited swampland, fifteen miles west of New Madrid in the Louisiana Territory (now Missouri).

In 1767, Charles Mason had noted in his journal: "The land in the forks of the Mississippi [River] is very good. Here it is much to be wished there was a Settlement. The climate and the Soil invite every Stranger's Stay." The land may have been very good,

Settlers arrive in Cincinnati by covered wagon or by flatboat down the Ohio River.

but not many strangers lingered at the poor little New Madrid settlement that developed just south of "the forks of the Mississippi." First an Indian camp and then a Spanish colony, tumble-down New Madrid was only a short distance from the western end of Mason and Dixon's line, where the Ohio River flowed into the Mississippi.

An 1810 visitor to New Madrid observed: "The men mostly follow boating, and the women, during their absence, make out to raise a little corn to keep themselves alive until the return of their husbands, when they drink and dance as long as their money lasts." Another visitor commented: "They have plenty of cattle,

A poor woodcutter and his family lead a hard life on the banks of the Mississippi River.

but seem in other respects to be very poor. . . . There is a church going to decay and no preacher."

Poor or not, New Madrid was about to become world-famous, at least in scientific circles. "About two o'clock this morning we were awakened by a most tremendous noise, while the house danced about and seemed as if it would fall on our heads," wrote a New Madrid woman, describing the first shock of what would forever after be called the New Madrid Earthquakes. With more shocks weakening their already shaky log cabins, the people of New Madrid fled their homes in panic.

An eyewitness recounted that at 7 A.M. "the danger was increased by another shock, which racked the houses violently and threw down the chimneys. The darkness returned, and it was accompanied by loud noises, and a bounding up and down motion." Another person told of the "many sparks of fire emitted from the earth," while still another reported that when the shocks "were at the severest point of their motion the people were thrown on the ground at almost every step. . . . The earth was observed to roll in waves a few feet high."

Underground water forced up through the earth blew into the air "with loud explosions . . . to the height of ten to fifteen feet, and fell back in a black shower." As the New Madrid waterfront streets and graveyard simply slid into the Mississippi River and disappeared, what trees were still left bent toward the ground, then snapped upright, their branches interlocking. Because the New Madrid buildings were log structures that had enough flexibility to move and sway with the shocks, only one life was lost, that of a terrified woman who ran until she died of heart failure.

The New Madrid shocks continued on and off all through that winter, with the intensity of the shocks on January 23, 1812, and on February 7, 1812, equal to the first. In the three months between December 16, 1811, and March 15, 1812, an engineer living in Louisville, some 270 miles from New Madrid, recorded 1,874 separate shocks. When shocks hit during the daytime, smoke or fog darkened the air for several hours afterwards, while vapors rising from the fissures, or openings in the earth, had a burning brimstone or rotten egg smell, making the water unfit to drink for a distance of 150 miles.

When the shocks hit at night, weird lights and flashes that resembled explosions of gas or lightning were seen low on the horizon. The sounds were equally frightening: "a thousand pieces of artillery going off" . . . "an awful noise resembling loud and distant thunder" . . . "explosions and a terrible mixture of noises."

Although New Madrid had originally been built fifteen to twenty feet above the flood level of the Mississippi River, it sank so low during the earthquakes that the entire village was under five feet of water following the spring floods of 1812. A boatman who stopped at New Madrid in March 1812 reported that he "found the place a complete wreck, sunk about twelve feet below its level, and entirely deserted." The people of New Madrid had long since retreated to an open field behind town where they were living in tents or makeshift huts and cooking over campfires.

Travelers on the Ohio and Mississippi rivers during the quakes recounted their own tales of terror. "I could distinctly see the river agitated as if by a storm; and although the noise was inconceivably loud and terrific, I could distinctly hear the crash of falling trees, and the screaming of the wild fowl on the river," a flatboat passenger recalled. "The river was literally covered with the wrecks of boats," reported an eyewitness. "Boats with their crews were engulfed and never more heard of," declared a riverboatman.

The artist and naturalist, John James Audubon, described his experience 150 miles from New Madrid on the banks of the Ohio River in Kentucky: "The ground rose and fell in billows like the ruffled waters of a lake. . . . I heard what I imagined to be the distant rumbling of a violent tornado . . . shock succeeded shock almost every day or night for several weeks. . . . The earth waved like a field of corn before the breeze: the birds left their perches, and flew about not knowing whither."

More than 700 miles away, in Washington, D.C., the shock "was considerable enough to shake the doors and windows, and wake persons from their sleep." In Richmond, Virginia, people

The people of New Madrid flee their homes in terror when the first earthquake hits.

"staggered where they stood," while in Charleston, South Carolina, "The agitation of the earth was such that the bells in the church steeples rang." During the February 7, 1812, quake, a Congressman testified that in Pittsburgh "many persons were so much alarmed as to rise from their beds and run out of doors, screaming with affright."

It was no wonder that accounts came from all over the country. An area of one million square miles could feel the vibrations without instruments, while the strongest of the shocks could be felt from Quebec, Canada, to the Gulf of Mexico and from the Rocky Mountains to the Atlantic Seaboard. More than 150,000 acres of forest were destroyed, while the course of the Mississippi River was permanently changed for 140 miles. Opposite New Madrid in Tennessee, brand-new Reelfoot Lake was formed over what had once been woodlands. With the tremors continuing for more than two years, as late as December 1813, people in the Illinois Territory reported that during an aftershock "their stomachs were troubled with nausea and sometimes vomiting."

On a scale of I to XII, the National Oceanic and Atmospheric Administration gave the December 16th, January 23rd and February 7th New Madrid earthquakes its highest rating of XII, with XII described as: "Damage *total*. Waves seen on ground surfaces. Lines of sight and level distorted. Objects thrown upward in the air." Although the San Francisco earthquake of 1906 was rated lower, an XI, as a densely populated city, San Francisco sustained far more loss of life and property than did sparsely settled New Madrid.

Little loss of life and property or not, seismologists (scientists concerned with the study of earthquakes) classify the New Madrid earthquakes as the most severe ever recorded on the North American continent. Over the years, Mason and Dixon's line had been the scene of quarrels, massacres and wars between peoples and nations. But in the end, everyone everywhere, friend and foe alike, was powerless in the face of what nature unleashed along Mason and Dixon's line in that astonishing year of 1811.

The waters of the Ohio and Mississippi rivers become too turbulent to navigate during the New Madrid earthquakes.

CHAPTER 9

HALF SLAVE, HALF FREE

Charles Mason had predicted correctly that if the boundary line that he and Jeremiah Dixon surveyed was continued west along the Ohio River, it would fall on the "forks of the Mississippi." What Mason hadn't predicted, and couldn't have predicted, was that their line would become a dividing line between North and South. As Mason and Dixon's line followed the course of the Ohio River, the states and territories south of the line were all slaveholding, while the states and territories north of the line were free.

Up until 1818, an equal balance of free and slave states (eleven of each) had kept peace between the North and South. But in 1818, Missouri applied for statehood . . . as a slave state. There was an immediate uproar in Congress, followed by two years of bitter debate. Concerned by the furious arguments over slavery, former President Thomas Jefferson wrote: "This momentous question, like a fire bell in the night, awakened and filled me with terror."

At last, in 1820, Congress passed the Missouri Compromise that preserved the balance by admitting Missouri as a slave state and Maine as a free state. The Compromise also stated that, with the exception of Missouri, slavery would be forbidden in all the territory north of latitude 36 degrees 30 minutes. That parallel of latitude, which was the southern border of Missouri, was only a few miles from the village of New Madrid, which had been rebuilt farther inland after the earthquakes. By terms of the Missouri Compromise of 1820, Mason and Dixon's line of division between free and slave ran all the way from the Delaware River to the Rocky Mountains.

In the early years of the Republic, slave owners made excuses for slavery as an evil necessary for their economy. But two slave uprisings, one in 1822 by a free black, Denmark Vesey, and one in 1831 led by the slave Nat Turner in which fifty-seven whites were

After 1820, Mason and Dixon's line divides the country into free and slave.

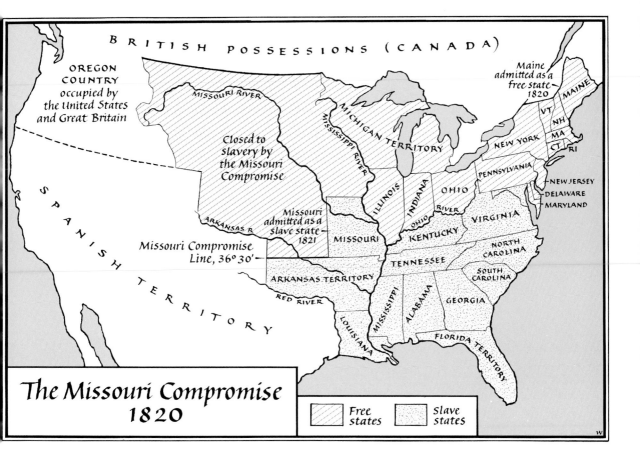

The Missouri Compromise 1820

OREGON COUNTRY occupied by the United States and Great Britain

BRITISH POSSESSIONS (CANADA)

Maine admitted as a free state 1820

SPANISH TERRITORY

MISSOURI RIVER

Closed to slavery by the Missouri Compromise

ARKANSAS R.

Missouri Compromise Line, 36° 30'

Missouri admitted as a slave state 1821

ARKANSAS TERRITORY

RED RIVER

LOUISIANA

MISSISSIPPI RIVER

MICHIGAN TERRITORY

ILLINOIS

INDIANA

OHIO

OHIO RIVER

MISSOURI

KENTUCKY

TENNESSEE

MISSISSIPPI

ALABAMA

GEORGIA

FLORIDA TERRITORY

NEW YORK

PENNSYLVANIA

VIRGINIA

NORTH CAROLINA

SOUTH CAROLINA

VT

NH

MA

CT

RI

MAINE

NEW JERSEY

DELAWARE

MARYLAND

Free states   Slave states

killed, hardened southern attitudes. The southern writer George Fitzhugh declared that slave owners "became convinced that slavery was morally right, that it would continue ever to exist, that it was as profitable as it was humane."

North of Mason and Dixon's line attitudes hardened, too. In an attempt to stir up public opinion against slavery, those people who demanded that all slavery be abolished, called abolitionists, lectured, traveled and wrote articles and books. Abolitionists also played an important role in the Underground Railroad that assisted some thirty to forty thousand slaves escape over Mason and Dixon's line from the slave South to the free North.

The Underground Railroad wasn't a real railroad, but a network of paths, roads, streams and rivers that all led north. The slaves were called "passengers," the men and women who led the slaves to safety, "conductors," and the buildings where the slaves were hidden, "stations." Free blacks and former slaves were key figures in running the Underground Railroad, acting as conductors and providing shelter, food, clothing and assistance to fugitive slaves. Although only a small percentage of slaves ever escaped, the impact of the Underground Railroad was enormous. In the South it enraged slave owners, while in the North, it united free blacks, former slaves and abolitionists in a common goal.

Pennsylvania's Brandywine Valley, which had been the site of Mason and Dixon's headquarters, and where George Washington had been defeated by the British in 1777, was a major throughway for runaway slaves. Quakers, who traditionally opposed slavery, ran an active Underground Railroad for slaves fleeing over Mason and Dixon's line from the neighboring slave states of Maryland and Delaware. The village of Kennett Square, where the British Army had assembled before the Battle of the Brandywine, was known as a "hotbed of abolitionists." Former slave Harriet Tubman, who was called "the Moses of her People," often worked as a conductor out of the Kennett Square area, funneling runaway slaves through Wilmington, Delaware, and from there, over Mason and Dixon's line into Pennsylvania.

In Columbia, Pennsylvania, there was a large settlement of for-

An escaped slave herself, Harriet Tubman leads hundreds of runaways over Mason and Dixon's line to freedom.

mer slaves who had gained their freedom legally. For many years William Whipper, a former slave, helped hundreds of fugitives escape to the settlement which became a refuge for runaways. Whipper described the bridge that had been built over the Susquehanna River at the site of Thomas Cresap's old ferry line: "The long bridge connecting Wrightsville with Columbia, was the only safe outlet by which they [the runaways] could successfully escape their pursuers," he wrote. "When they had crossed this bridge they could look back . . . and say to the slave power: 'Thus far shalt thou come, and no farther.'"

By no means limited to Pennsylvania, the Underground Railroad ran the full length of Mason and Dixon's line along the Ohio River, with numerous stations in Ohio, Indiana and Illinois. Over a period of thirty-five years, Levi Coffin and his wife forwarded more than two thousand slaves through their Indiana home. Coffin, who was unofficially known as the president of the Underground Railroad, noted: "Three principal lines from the South converged at our house. The Roads were always in running order, the connections were good, the conductors active and zealous, and there was no lack of passengers."

But in the end, it was the slaves themselves who had to take that first courageous step toward freedom. In 1842, former slave Moses Grandy described the risks: "They hide themselves, during the day, in the woods or swamps; at night, they travel, crossing rivers by swimming or by boats they may chance to meet with, and passing over hills and meadows which they do not know: in these dangerous journeys they are guided by the north-star, for they know only that the land of freedom is in the north."

Mason and Dixon's line was every runaway's goal. Harriet Tubman recounted her reaction to stepping over Mason and Dixon's line. "I had crossed the line of which I had so long been dreaming. I was free. . . . There was such a glory over everything; the sun came through like gold through the trees and over the fields, and I felt like I was in Heaven." A fugitive slave recalled, "Face, eyes, hopes, and steps, were set as flint. What time the following day we crossed Mason and Dixon's line is not recorded on the Underground Railroad books." Another fugitive wrote how he had been captured because he thought that he was "several miles across Mason and Dixon's Line, but I was evidently yet in the state of Maryland."

Up until 1850, northern personal freedom laws made finding and recovering runaway slaves almost impossible for southern slave holders. But in 1850, at a time when the white population of the South was about 6,250,000 and the slave population was something over 3,000,000, Congress enacted the Compromise of 1850. One of the Compromise's five provisions was a harsh new Fugitive Slave law. No matter how long a slave had been free, that slave could be seized with "such reasonable force and restraint as may be necessary." The slave could then be shipped South without a trial by jury or the right to testify in his or her own behalf in court.

Because the new law allowed federal marshals and professional slave catchers to hunt fugitives north of Mason and Dixon's line, after 1850 there was no safe hiding place for runaways in the United States. "I wouldn't trust Uncle Sam with my people any

Even this free man isn't safe after the Fugitive Slave law is passed in 1850.

longer but I brought them clear all the way to Canada," Harriet Tubman declared after passage of the new law.

The law also stated that "any persons who shall knowingly or willingly obstruct, hinder, or prevent" an arrest would be fined, jailed or both. Abolitionist-writer Ralph Waldo Emerson was outraged, denouncing the law as a "filthy enactment . . . I will not obey it, by God!" Others wouldn't obey it either. A year after the Fugitive Slave Law was passed, a Philadelphia newspaper reported: "Last Thursday morning, a peaceful neighborhood in the borders of Lancaster county, was made the scene of a bloody battle."

On September 11, 1851, fugitive slaves hiding in a safe "station" just north of Mason and Dixon's line in Christiana, Pennsylvania, had been surrounded by a band of southern slave catchers. The slaves opened fire from inside the house, wounding a constable and the slave owner's son and killing the slave owner, who had earlier said that he would "go to hell, or have his slaves." Although free blacks in the neighborhood had immediately rallied to help defend the "station," the governor called in the militia, and the rebellion was quickly crushed.

The runaways, plus the free blacks who had come to their aid, were thrown in the Lancaster County jail. (Lancaster had built a new jail since the days of Sheriff Smith and the Paxton Boys.) Thanks to a brilliant defense by abolitionist lawyers, all twenty-seven blacks and three white sympathizers were found Not Guilty. The verdict, which infuriated the South, gave new hope in the North to both runaways and abolitionists.

Eight years later, John Brown, a fiery abolitionist, his two sons, fourteen whites and five blacks crossed Mason and Dixon's line from Pennsylvania into slaveholding Virginia. As the first step in the creation of a fugitive slave stronghold in the nearby mountains, Brown and his comrades raided the armory at Harpers Ferry, Virginia, on October 16, 1859. Their objective was to steal guns from the armory to use in a violent overthrow of slavery. (George Washington had surveyed the area as a young man and recommended Harpers Ferry as "the most eligible spot on the

[Potomac] river" for an armory. The armory had been built in 1796 during Washington's second term as President.)

By the next day, October 17, the rioters had holed up in the Harpers Ferry fire engine house, captured some forty hostages and killed four townspeople, including the mayor, all the while holding off the state militia. Not until October 18, when the U.S. Marines, led by Colonel Robert E. Lee, stormed the fire engine house, was the insurrection put down. Although the wounded John Brown survived, both his sons and thirteen of the rebels were killed. Brown was immediately tried, convicted of treason and sentenced to hang. On the day he was to die, a still-defiant Brown declared to the nation that if he had another chance, he

A fighting John Brown tries to abolish slavery by violent means.

would again "mingle my blood further with the blood of my children and with the blood of millions in the slave country."

The two riots, the Christiana riot north of Mason and Dixon's line in Pennsylvania, and John Brown's insurrection south of Mason and Dixon's line in Virginia, electrified the country. Although both outbreaks had been short-lived, they demonstrated to the country how close violence was to the national surface.

"A house divided against itself cannot stand," Abraham Lincoln declared during his 1858 Senate race in a quotation from the Bible. "I believe this government cannot endure permanently half slave and half free." And it couldn't. Mason and Dixon's line no longer marked a border between free and slave. It had severed the country in two.

A slave symbolically breaks his chains as he crosses Mason and Dixon's line.

CHAPTER 10

AN ORDINARY LITTLE TOWN

As the 1860s began, Gettysburg, Pennsylvania, was just an ordinary little country town of 2,400 people seven miles north of Mason and Dixon's line. Surrounded by a rich patchwork of fields and orchards, Gettysburg, which had been known as Marsh Creek Settlement during the time of Mason and Dixon's survey, prided itself on a small college and a seminary for training ministers. Ten roads led in and out of town, making it a natural market center for neighboring farms.

Ordinary or not, the outbreak of the Civil War would write the name of Gettysburg in the world's history books and change the sleepy little village forever. The Civil War, which had begun in April 1861, was fought between the Confederate States of America and the United States government. The eleven southern states that made up the Confederacy were determined to be an independent nation, while the federal government, represented by the free states north of Mason and Dixon's line, was equally determined to reunite the country.

Although the slave states that bordered Mason and Dixon's line to the south, Delaware, Maryland, Kentucky and Missouri, had strong ties to both the North and the South, in the end they remained loyal to the Union. On the other hand, the border slave state of Virginia seceded, or withdrew, from the Union and joined the Confederacy as soon as war broke out. Because the Virginia counties west of the Allegheny Mountains had nothing in common with Virginia's eastern counties, including slavery, they formed their own government. The free state of West Virginia was admitted to the Union in June 1863.

During that same month of June 1863, Confederate General Robert E. Lee made a fateful decision to invade Pennsylvania. Like British General William Howe, who had believed that an invasion of Pennsylvania would be a turning point for the British in the American Revolution, General Lee believed that a victory in Pennsylvania would be a turning point for the Confederacy in the Civil War. Besides, Pennsylvania's rich farmlands and manufacturing centers would provide much-needed food and supplies for his rebel troops. Lee, who had led the Marine unit that had crushed John Brown's rebellion at Harpers Ferry in 1859, was unfailingly soft-spoken and morally courageous. Furthermore, he was an aggressive military leader who was idolized by his soldiers. General Stonewall Jackson spoke for all of Lee's men when he declared, "I would follow him blindfolded."

Fresh from a victory over the Union Army at Chancellorsville, Virginia, Lee led his Army of Northern Virginia, some 70,000 to 75,000 men, from Virginia into Maryland on June 14, 1863. The rebel army marched through Maryland and crossed Mason and Dixon's line into Pennsylvania, where Lee planned to take a stand at South Mountain. Mason and Dixon knew the territory well. "Continued the line. Crossed Toms Creek at the foot of the South Mountain," Mason had written in August of 1765.

Crossing Mason and Dixon's line was a memorable event for some of Lee's soldiers. "Jim Crow, Van Whitehead and I persuaded an old gentleman to show us exactly where the line ran and then standing with one foot in Maryland and the other in

Confederate General Robert E. Lee rides into battle on his famous horse, Traveller.

Pennsylvania, we finished the contents of a canteen, drinking some pretty heavy toasts," bragged a rebel corporal.

At the approach of Lee's forces, Pennsylvania was in an uproar. "The people look as sour as vinegar and, I have no doubt, would gladly send us all to Kingdom come if they could," penned a Confederate officer in a letter home. The sour looks were understandable. As Lee's troops marched across Pennsylvania, they helped themselves to cattle, horses, pigs, produce, clothing and supplies. "Fowls and pigs and eatables don't stand much chance," admitted a rebel soldier.

With only a small company of militia to protect them, the people of Gettysburg were in an uproar, too, as well they might have been. On June 26, Confederate troops brushed aside the militia like so many pesky mosquitoes and invaded Gettysburg. "What a horrible sight!" declared a fifteen-year-old Gettysburg schoolgirl. "There they were, human beings! clad almost in rags, covered with dust, riding pell-mell down the hill toward our home! shouting, yelling most unearthly, cursing, brandishing their revolvers, and firing right and left!"

Gettysburg had a constable, John Burns, but he was old, old enough to have served in the War of 1812 and the Mexican War, and much too old to have been accepted by the Union Army when he tried to enlist. Nevertheless, as the Confederate troops prepared to bed down in the town square that night, John Burns appeared with his "long brown rifle" and announced that they were all under arrest for trespassing on United States property. The soldiers just laughed and locked the old man up in his own jail where he remained until the troops rode out of Gettysburg the next morning.

Breathing a sigh of relief at the Confederates' departure, the people of Gettysburg released John Burns from jail and returned to tending their farms. "The Rebels burned the railroad bridge and a few cars," a Gettysburg citizen wrote. "Besides this, they did not do much damage in the town."

Meanwhile, unknown to either the people of Gettysburg or to

General Lee, the Union Army of the Potomac, over 90,000 strong, had been steadily marching north. After the Union defeat at Chancellorsville, Virginia, President Abraham Lincoln had appointed George Meade as the new commander of the Union Army of the Potomac. Tough, short-tempered and capable, Meade knew, and didn't care, that his men called him a "damned goggle-eyed snapping turtle." Leading his army out of Virginia, Meade made plans to take his stand against Lee just south of Mason and Dixon's line near Taneytown, Maryland.

Meade's first order of business on reaching Taneytown was to send a division of cavalry into Pennsylvania to check on the enemy forces and report their whereabouts back to him. When the people of Gettysburg saw a cloud of dust approaching up the Emmitsburg Road from Maryland on June 28, they were elated. It must be Union soldiers, friends, not foes! A young man recalled, "I well remember how secure this made us feel. We thought surely now we were safe."

By this time, the southern troops had already captured the Pennsylvania towns of Chambersburg, York, Carlisle and even little Wrightsville, the site of Thomas Cresap's ferry service during the Conojacular War. To ward off a possible rebel attack on Pennsylvania's capital at Harrisburg, northern militiamen had burned down the Susquehanna River bridge that linked Wrightsville and Columbia, the bridge that for decades had been a gateway to freedom for runaway slaves.

On the same day that Meade's cavalry rode toward Gettysburg, a spy arrived at General Lee's headquarters, located northwest of Gettysburg in Chambersburg, with alarming news. General Meade's Union army was close, closer than most of Lee's own rebel corps, which were still scattered across the Pennsylvania countryside. Never one to underestimate an opponent, Lee announced, "General Meade will make no blunder on my front."

Lee's orders went out . . . forget capturing Harrisburg . . . return on the double . . . a battle is looming. Although Gettysburg was a battleground that neither general had chosen, all ten roads,

like the spokes in a wheel, converged on the little village. "We know how straight into the very jaws of destruction and death leads this road to Gettysburg," a troubled Confederate officer wrote.

Not everyone was worried. Confederate General Henry Heth, who was also stationed in Chambersburg, was more concerned about finding shoes for his men. Hearing that there was a supply of shoes in Gettysburg (there wasn't), Heth made a request of his commanding officer. Despite the presence of a small northern cavalry troop camped on the outskirts of town, was there any objection to Heth marching his men into Gettysburg to pick up some badly needed shoes? "No objection in the world," Heth's commanding officer responded, and with that offhand reply, the fate of two armies, and Gettysburg, was sealed.

On their way into Gettysburg early the next morning, General Heth's Confederate infantry division ran into the Union cavalry about two miles out of town on the Chambersburg Road. Because the cavalry, which was traditionally supposed to fight only a delaying action, was never a match for the infantry, the encounter promised to be a routine skirmish. But on this hot and dusty July first morning, the skirmish that developed wasn't routine. And there would be no new shoes for anyone.

As the day wore on, divisions of Meade's infantry came marching up the Emmitsburg Road from Maryland. Meanwhile, Lee's troops, which were assembling from all over Pennsylvania, thundered toward Gettysburg. By noon the hilly ridge west of town by the seminary had become the site of a major battle. A Union gunner recalled "bullets hissing, humming and whistling everywhere; cannon roaring; all crash on crash and peal on peal, smoke, dust, splinters, blood, wreck and carnage indescribable."

Although Constable John Burns had grabbed his ancient rifle and run to the scene of the battle, he had been ordered back by the Union soldiers. "I know how to fight. I've fit before," Burns retorted. When the soldiers saw how determined the old man was, they gave him a rifle from a fallen comrade and let him join the

General George Meade is President Abraham Lincoln's choice to be the new commander of the Union Army of the Potomac.

The bloody battle of Gettysburg results in thousands of deaths.

Pennsylvania Volunteers. "I never saw John Burns after our movement to the right," recalled a Union soldier. "I only know that he was true blue and grit to the backbone, and fought until he was three times wounded."

By late afternoon, the Union troops were in full retreat. Lieutenant Frank Haskell described their flight through the streets of Gettysburg: "Back in disorganized masses they fled into the town, hotly pursued, and in lanes, in barns, in yards and cellars, throwing away their arms, they sought to hide like rabbits, and were there captured, unresisting, by hundreds."

But the Union forces were far from defeated. After retreating

through Gettysburg, they took a stand on the long ridge and high ground east of town where the battle continued to rage. The fighting tipped first one way and then another through July second and third. It wasn't until late afternoon on July third that the Union forces finally emerged victorious in the bloodiest battle of this country's bloodiest war. "All was silent there," Lieutenant Haskell commented. "The wounded horses were limping about the field; the ravages of the conflict were still fearfully visible—the scattered arms and the ground thickly dotted with the dead."

Ironically, that awesome battle had been fought in such commonplace settings as the Peach Orchard, the Wheatfield, Plum

Run, Pitzer Woods. With so much of the fighting close to the town itself, it seemed miraculous that the only civilian death in Gettysburg had been a young woman shot by a stray bullet, while Constable John Burns survived his wounds to live nine more years.

Some one hundred years after Colonel George Washington had ordered a July fourth retreat from Fort Necessity along Mason and Dixon's line, General Robert E. Lee ordered a July fourth retreat along the same line. His defeated troops, as well as a seventeen-mile-long wagon train of ambulances and farm wagons filled with thousands of the wounded and dying, withdrew from Gettysburg during a drenching downpour. Although the Civil War would drag on for another two years, the turning point had been reached at Gettysburg, not for the South as Lee had anticipated, but for the North, in the most important battle of the war. During those unforgettable three days, more than 51,000 men had been killed, wounded, captured or were missing. The whole country was stunned by the number of casualties, and Gettysburg suddenly symbolized the terrible toll that the war was taking on America's young men.

What possible sense could be made of such madness? One suggestion was to dedicate a national cemetery at Gettysburg for the war dead. On November 19, 1863, over 15,000 people gathered in Gettysburg for the ceremonies. After the main speaker had finished a two-hour oration, President Abraham Lincoln, who had been asked to make a "few appropriate remarks," spoke for two minutes. In his rather high-pitched voice, the President finally made sense out of the tragedy that had been Gettysburg.

The Civil War has been a test, Lincoln said, as to whether this nation and its dream of liberty and freedom for all of its people can survive. The men who fought and died here, northerners and southerners alike, gave their utmost for that cause of freedom. Now it is time for the living to carry on the struggle so that "government of the people, by the people, for the people shall not perish from the earth."

After the battle, Constable John Burns poses outside his Gettysburg home with his rifle and his crutches.

A young Michigan private is a member of the 4th Michigan regiment, which suffers heavy casualties at Gettysburg.

President Abraham Lincoln states the great principles of the Union in his Gettysburg Address.

If such a momentous battle had to be fought, perhaps it was fitting that it should have been fought along Mason and Dixon's line that had split the nation between free and slave. And if anyone was to elevate Gettysburg's fiery battleground into a national shrine for freedom, it was also fitting that the President who ultimately reunited the country should be the one to do it.

CHAPTER II

"THE TIES THAT BIND"

The year 1865 brought an end of the Civil War but it by no means brought an end to the hostility between North and South. President Abraham Lincoln had promised "With malice toward none, with charity for all . . . to bind up the nation's wounds." But just days after Confederate General Robert E. Lee surrendered on April 9, 1865, Lincoln was assassinated. Twelve bitter years of Reconstruction followed, as Congress divided the southern states into military districts. It wasn't until 1877 that the last of the federal troops were withdrawn from the South.

Although healing of such deep wounds was painfully slow, the 1880s witnessed a beginning, at least economically. And it was appropriate that the healing should start along Mason and Dixon's line. As the United States moved from an agricultural to an industrial society after the Civil War, the whole country became increasingly dependent on railroads to move freight and people. At the end of the Civil War in 1865, there were 35,000 miles of railroad

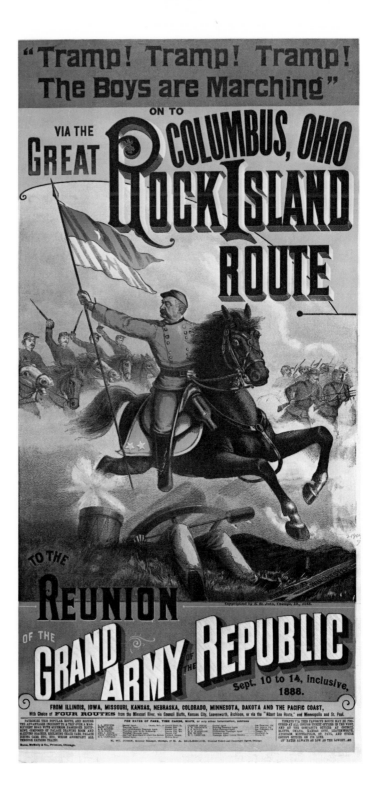

At a time when most of America moves by train, a railroad poster advertises a reunion of Civil War veterans in Denver.

track in the United States, while by 1880, there were 93,000 miles.

But not all of the tracks had the same gauge, gauge being the distance between the two rails. Most of the major railroad lines north of Mason and Dixon's line had a standard track gauge of four feet eight and a half inches. The standard gauge was copied from the British who, in turn, had retained the four-feet-eight-and-a-half-inch gauge used on coal-mining carts during the Roman occupation of Britain in the first century.

South of Mason and Dixon's line the track gauge measured five feet. All of a railroad company's rolling stock, which was its freight, passenger and repair cars, had wheels with the same gauge as the tracks it ran on. It goes without saying that rolling stock couldn't travel on tracks that had a wider or narrower gauge. That northern and southern railroad lines had different-width gauges caused long and expensive delays for trains that traveled across Mason and Dixon's line.

By 1880, over 11 percent of the tracks in the country had a gauge of five feet, and all those tracks were south of Mason and Dixon's line and east of the Mississippi River. Because the South had stubbornly continued to build railroad tracks with a five-foot gauge throughout the Civil War and Reconstruction years, the South had added 5,000 miles of five-foot-gauge track between 1860 and 1880. When a number of railroad bridges with standard-gauge tracks were built in the 1870s over the Ohio River (still considered to be Mason and Dixon's line), several southern railroad companies with trains that crossed the Ohio River voluntarily switched to standard gauge.

That still left some 13,000 miles of southern track with a five-foot gauge. Because travel between North and South across Mason and Dixon's line was becoming an increasing financial burden, the southern railroads finally agreed to take action. On February 2, 1886, representatives from all the important southern lines met to discuss a plan for switching their lines over to a narrower gauge.

May 31 and June 1, 1886, were selected as the two days when all the southern tracks would be changed. On the two switchover days, all traffic was halted as three-man track gangs were assigned to every mile of track, except on bridges, trestles or curves, which were handled by five men. Work both days began at exactly 3 A.M. and ended at 4 P.M., with people traveling great distances to watch the track crews compete for time records. The winners were a foreman and his crew on the Louisville & Nashville line who changed over eleven miles of track in four and a half hours. Because the gauge on the wheels of all the rolling stock had to be changed, too, the final cost of the switchover amounted to about $150 a mile.

At 4 P.M. on June 1, 1886, train traffic was resumed and the American railroad system became an interchangeable network for the first time in history. People and freight could now be transported between North and South across Mason and Dixon's line without costly delays or makeshift arrangements. The *Railroad Gazette* reported: "Passenger or freight cars could leave Portland, Maine, or Portland, Oregon; San Francisco, Chicago, or any prominent railway centre, and traverse without change of trucks or bulk every mile of southern road leading to New Orleans, Texas, or Florida."

Certainly unifying the railroads across Mason and Dixon's line didn't solve all the problems between North and South. But it was a first step toward "binding up the nation's wounds." The quarrels and disputes that had arisen between Lord Baltimore and William Penn two hundred years earlier had at last ended.

During those same two hundred years, both Mason and Dixon's line, and the country, had served as a battleground for violence, from early colonial boundary disputes to natural disasters to the holocaust that was the Civil War. Well-known figures had left their imprint on that historic line, William Penn, Lord Baltimore, George Washington, Chief Pontiac, Charles Mason, Jeremiah Dixon, the Marquis de Lafayette, Alexander Hamilton, Harriet Tubman, John Brown, Robert E. Lee, George Meade, Abraham Lincoln.

Thousands of nameless Americans had left their imprint, too, settlers, frontiersmen, native Americans, riverboatmen, slaves and foot soldiers. Today Mason and Dixon's line is no longer a battle-ground on which conflict rages. Instead it has become a symbolic landmark pointing to our country's stormy beginnings, restless growth, bitter divisions and ultimate survival.

A contemporary cartoon shows how the same gauge of track unites the North and the South on June 1, 1886.

Abbott, W. W., ed. *The Papers of George Washington.* "Colonial Series," Volume I. Charlottesville: University Press of Virginia, 1983.

Audubon, John James. *Delineations of American Scenery and Character.* New York: G. A. Baker & Company, 1926.

Bailey, Kenneth P. *Thomas Cresap: Maryland Frontiersman.* Boston: The Christopher Publishing House, 1944.

Baldwin, Leland D. *Whiskey Rebels.* Pittsburgh: University of Pittsburgh Press, 1939.

Brackenridge, H. H. *Incidents of the Insurrection.* New Haven, Conn.: College & University Press, 1795. (Reprint 1972)

Bradford, Sarah H. *Harriet: the Moses of Her People.* New York: G. R. Lockwood & Son, 1886.

Buck, Solon J., and Elizabeth H. Buck. *The Planting of Civilization in Western Pennsylvania.* Pittsburgh: University of Pittsburgh Press, 1939.

Carson, Gerald. "A Tax on Whiskey? Never!" *American Heritage,* August 1963, Volume XIV, Number 5. New York: American Heritage Publishing Co., p. 62ff.

Catton, Bruce, narrated by, *The American Heritage Picture History of the Civil War.* New York: American Heritage Publishing Co., 1960.

Catton, Bruce, *Gettysburg: The Final Fury.* Garden City, New York: Doubleday & Company, 1974.

Commager, Henry Steele, ed. *Documents of American History.* New York: Appleton-Century-Crofts, 1968.

Commager, Henry Steele, and Richard B. Morris, ed. *The Spirit of 'Seventy-Six.* New York: Harper & Row, Publishers, 1958.

Cope, Thomas D. *The Scientific Monthly.* "Charles Mason and Jeremiah Dixon," Volume LXII, No. 6. June 1946.

Davison, Charles. *Great Earthquakes.* London: Thomas Murby & Co., 1936.

Earthquake History of the United States. Boulder, Colorado: United States Department of Commerce, 1970.

Fisher, Sydney George. *Pennsylvania: Colony and Commonwealth.* Philadelphia: Henry T. Coates and Company, MDCCXCVII.

Fitzpatrick, John C., ed. *The Writings of George Washington from the Original Manuscript Sources 1745–1799*, Volume 1. Washington: United States Printing Office, 1931.

Foote, Shelby. *The Civil War: A Narrative,* Volume II. New York: Random Houses, 1963.

Flexner, James T. *George Washington: Anguish and Farewell.* Boston: Little, Brown and Company, 1969.

Flexner, James T. *George Washington: The Forge of Experience.* Boston: Little, Brown and Company, 1965.

Freeman, Douglas Southall. *George Washington: A Biography.* "Young Washington," Volume One. New York: Charles Scribner's Sons, 1948.

Fuller, Myron L. *The New Madrid Earthquake.* Department of the Interior, United States Geological Survey Bulletin 494, Washington: Government Printing Office, 1912.

Gara, Larry. *The Liberty Line.* Lexington: University of Kentucky Press, 1961.

Garrett, Wilbur E., ed. *Historical Atlas of the United States.* Washington, D.C.: National Geographic Society, 1988.

Harwell, Richard B., ed. *The War They Fought.* New York: Longmans, Green and Co., 1960.

Illick, Joseph E. *Colonial Pennsylvania: A History.* New York: Charles Scribner's Sons, 1976.

Jackson, Donald, and Dorothy Twohig, eds. *The Diaries of George Washington,* Volume VI. Charlottesville: University Press of Virginia, 1979.

Kraus, Michael. *The United States to 1865.* Ann Arbor: The University of Michigan Press, 1959.

Latrobe, John H. B. *The History of Mason and Dixon's Line.* Press of the Historical Society of Pennsylvania, 1854.

The Life, Trial and Execution of Captain John Brown, Compiled from official and Authentic Sources. New York: Robert M. DeWitt, Publisher, 1859.

Lowdermilk, Will H. *History of Cumberland (Maryland).* Baltimore: Regional Publishing Company, 1878.

Marrin, Albert. *Struggle for a Continent: The French and Indian Wars 1690–1760.* New York: Atheneum, 1987.

Marrin, Albert. *The War for Independence.* New York: Atheneum, 1988.

Mason, A. Hughlett, and William F. Swindler. "Mason & Dixon: Their Line and Its Legend." *American Heritage,* Volume XV, Number 2, February 1964. New York: American Heritage Publishing Company, 1967.

Mason, Charles. *The Journal of Charles Mason and Jeremiah Dixon*. Transcribed by the United States Archives. Philadelphia: American Philosophical Society, 1969.

Minutes of the Provincial Council of Pennsylvania, Volumes VI, VII, IX. Harrisburg: Theo. Fenn & Co., 1852.

Morison, Samuel Eliot, and Henry Steele Commager. *The Growth of the American Republic*. New York: Oxford University Press, 1962.

Newman, Joseph, ed. *200 Years: A Bicentennial Illustrated History of the United States*. Washington, D.C.: Books by U.S. News and World Report, 1975.

Penick, James L., Jr. *The New Madrid Earthquakes of 1811–1812*. Columbia, Missouri: University of Missouri Press, 1976.

Report on the Resurvey of the Maryland-Pennsylvania Boundary Part of the Mason and Dixon Line. Authorized by the Legislature of Maryland and Pennsylvania. Harrisburg, Pennsylvania: Harrisburg Publishing Co., State Printer, 1909.

Russell, Francis. *The French and Indian Wars*. New York: American Heritage Publishing Company, 1962.

Scharf, J. Thomas. *History of Maryland*, Volume I. Baltimore: John B. Piet, 1879.

Scheer, George F., and Hugh F. Rankin. *Rebels and Redcoats*. Cleveland: The World Publishing Company, 1957.

Slaughter, Thomas P. *The Whiskey Rebellion*. New York: Oxford University Press, 1986.

Still, William. *The Underground Rail Road*. Philadelphia: Porter & Coates, 1872.

Stotz, Charles. *Outposts of the War for Empire*. Pittsburgh: Historical Society of Western Pennsylvania, 1985.

Taylor, George Rogers, and Irene D. Neu. *The American Railroad Network, 1861–1890*. Cambridge, Massachusetts: Harvard University Press, 1956.

Thwaites, Reuben Gold. *Early Western Travels*, Volumes IV, V. Cleveland, Ohio: The Arthur H. Clark Company, 1904.

Van Every, Dale. *Forth to the Wilderness: The First American Frontier, 1754–1774*. New York: William Morrow and Company, 1961.

Ward, Christopher. *The War of the Revolution*, Volume I. New York: The Macmillan Company, 1952.

Wilson, William E. "Maryland, Their Maryland." *American Heritage,* Volume XVIII, Number 5. New York: American Heritage Publishing Company, 1967.

Wright, H. G. "The Mason and Dixon Line." *The Yale Review,* Volume XV, Number 4, July 1926.

Wroth, Lawrence C. *The Story of Thomas Cresap*. Columbia, Ohio: The Cresap Society, 1928.

INDEX

Page numbers in italics refer to illustrations.

Ohio River, 52, *75*, 85, 86, *87*, 88, 90, *92*, 94, 98, 117
Ohio Valley, 38
Old Hendrick, *56*
Old Town, Maryland, 20, 21, 23, 37, 40, 76, 81–82
Onondaga Indians, 55, 57
Ottawa Indians, 38

P

Paris, Treaty of, 38
Paxton Boys, 40, *41*, 47, 100
Penn, Richard, 42
Penn, Thomas, 42, 43
Penn, William, 14, 34, *35*, 42, 118
Penn family, 45, 50, 62
Philadelphia, Pennsylvania, 11, 19, 34, 40, 43, *43*, 44, 48, 62, 76, 82, 100
  in American Revolution, 66, 68, 73
Pitt, William, 37–38
Pittsburgh, Pennsylvania, 78, 93
Pontiac, 38, 40–41, 118
Pontiac's Rebellion, 38–41, 44
Proclamation of 1763, 52

R

Railroad Gazette, 118

S

San Francisco, California, 117
  earthquake of 1906, 93
Seneca Indians, 55, 59–60
Shawnee Indians, 20, 34, 39, 58–59
Shelby, Evan, 50, 51
Smith, Samuel, 18–19, 40, 47
Susquehanna River, *12*, 13, 18, 19, 34, 40, 47, 98, 107

T

Taneytown, Maryland, 107
Three Lower Counties, 44, 65,
Trimble's Ford, Pennsylvania, 69
Tubman, Harriet, 96, *97*, 98, 100, 118
Turner, Nat, 95–96

U

Underground Railroad, 96, 98–99

V

Vesey, Denmark, 95–96

W

Washington, George, 118
  in American Revolution, 66, 68–71, 73, 74, 76, 96
  in French and Indian War, 23–24, *25*, 26, 26–33, *32*, 35, 57, 112
  as president, 76, 79–83, 101
  as a surveyor, 21, *22*, 23, 100–101
  Whiskey Rebellion and, 76, 79–83, *83*
Washington, Pennsylvania, 59, 78
Whipper, William, 98
Whiskey Boys, 74, 76–83, *79*, *80*
Whiskey Rebellion, 74, 76–83
Whitehead, Van, 104, 106
Wills Creek, Maryland, 23, 24, 28, 29
Wrightsville/Wright's Ferry, Maryland/Pennsylvania, 13–14, 98, 107

Y

York, Pennsylvania, 73, 107

CREDITS

🗡

Maps on pages 2–3, 45, 69, 75, 84 and 95 are by Jeanyee Wong.

ILLUSTRATIONS

Albany Institute of History and Art, on loan from the Knox Family, p. 36

Atwater Kent Museum, p. 80

David L. Brill, © 1988, p. 52

Chicago Historical Society, p. 26

Enoch Pratt Free Library, p. 15

Library Company of Philadelphia, p. 43

Library of Congress, pp. 12, 17, 22, 27, 31, 32, 35, 41, 51, 56, 63, 64, 67, 71, 72, 79, 87, 88, 97, 99, 102, 105, 108, 110, 111, 114, 116, 119

Metropolitan Museum of Art, Gift of Edgar William and Bernice Chrysler Garbisch, 1963, p. 83

National Archives, pp. 10, 49, 61, 101, 113 (top and bottom)

National Archives of Canada, p. 36

New York Public Library, p. 77

Newberry Library, p. 39

Smithsonian Institution, p. 46

State Historical Society of Missouri, pp. 91, 92

Washington-Custis-Lee Collection, Washington and Lee University, p. 25